A Journey Through Words

Fr. Jim Tobin S.M.A

Dr. Caron Leid Editor

Copyright © 2023 Author Fr. Jim Tobin S.M.A

Editor Dr. Caron Leid

All rights reserved.

ISBN: 9798374835939

DEDICATION

I call him the human library, because you learn so much just by having a conversation with him and we have had many. He became a refuge for me . He will say he remembers me from St. Thomas Aquinas S.S, because he is too polite to hurt my feelings, (I know for sure, that he doesn't and it doesn't matter), because our closeness developed at the beginning of my mother's diagnosis of Alzheimer's disease, when I didn't know who to turn to other than my neighbour Fr. Tobin, a familiar face. I hadn't been a practicing Catholic but found hope taking my mom to church (when she could still participate) . I know many have stories with him and I am not alone with personal stories. He doesn't know, (well he will now), that he lessoned my grief, after my mom finally passed 20 years later, he was a constant, an open door , and a place of beautiful descriptive stories where you could envision every single scene. I will miss him so much , I hide my grief from him during his last weeks in Canada, because I know moving back to Ireland is what's best for him and one thing I have learnt from him, is his self-less nature, which I now have to emulate! The best tangible gift he has left me, are his homilies and I intend to publish every single one! This is volume 1.- What an honour!

ACKNOWLEDGMENTS

I would like to thank Fr. Tobin for being the person that
you can speak to about anything and renewing my faith,
maybe not religiously but definitely spiritually.

ORDAINED IN NEWRY

Fr. James Tobin, S.M.A., son of Mr. and Mrs. Jimmie Tobin, Graine, Urlingford, who was ordained in Newry Cathedral, on Wednesday by Most Most Rev. Dr. Crawford.

Fr. Tobin received his secondary education at the Sacred Heart College, Ballinafad, Co. Mayo, and graduated at University College, Cork. The Society has five houses in Ireland and about 500 Irish priests who are members of the Society are working in Nigeria, Ghana, Liberia and Egypt. An American Province has been started and there is now foundations in England and in Perth, W. Australia.

1

Sunday 23b.2015

You may've read Margery William's children's story,

The Velveteen Rabbit about toys becoming real by being loved for a long time: it tells us beautifully how people become real by being loved and cared for. Her Velveteen Rabbit story is about 100 years old: it's got to be more than 20 years since I last made use of it in a homily: many of you will recognize it!

"What is REAL?" asked the Rabbit one day, when they were lying side by side near the nursery fender, before Nana came to tidy the room:

"Does it mean having things that buzz inside you and a stick-out handle?"

"Real isn't how you are made," said the Skin Horse. "It's a thing that happens to you. When a child loves you for a long, long time, not just to play with, but REALLY loves you, then you become Real.". "Does it hurt?" asked the Rabbit. "Sometimes," said the Skin Horse, for he was always truthful. "When you are Real you don't mind being hurt." "Does it happen all at once, like being wound up," he asked, "or bit by bit?" "It doesn't happen all at once," said the Skin Horse. "You become. It takes a long time. That's why it doesn't happen often to people who break easily, or have sharp edges, or who must be carefully kept. Generally, by the time you are Real, most of your hair has been loved off & your eyes drop out and you get loose in the joints & very shabby. But these things don't matter at all, because once you are Real you can't be ugly, except to people who don't understand."

We often treat people as if they're unreal!

I think of this deaf man: I think of a story just before this; in Tyre, a gentile woman pleading with Jesus for her daughter & a strange exchange, Jesus, knowing how Jews despised gentiles, saying 'It is not fair to fake the children's food & throw it to the doss". It doesn't stop her. She says, "dogs are hungry too!" Even people thought of as doss, people on the other side of the line, without Torah, or Covenant, who are not considered "religious"! We she says, have needs too, our sick, our worries, all those things that trouble us in the middle of the night. We have our hungers, spiritual hungers too. We are real."

Her attitude moves Jesus. He has compassion for her, and He responds to her request by ridding her daughter of an unclean spirit; as he heals this man: he is still in Gentile territory, the Decapolis: so, we can assume he's a gentile: it really makes no difference to Jesus, what he is! In his expression of love towards the gentile woman & this deaf man both becomes real to him and to those around him that day. It's a story we need to hear good for this time of year. Just as Jesus hears the pleading of the deaf man's friends &responds, we are to be attentive to the cries for mercy from people we'd rather ignore or put labels on, so they become unreal to us!

The plight of many thousands of men, women, and children, especially the little ones, refugees from poverty & terror, is headline news - each day it seems to get worse: you may've seen on TV, or heard of, the 3-year-old boy drowned off the coast of Turkey earlier this week. It's an image hard to forget, but we forget! it's remote, removed from our safe world: let the Germans,

Italians, French, British - the Europeans, deal with it: it's on their doorstep, their problem: we can wash our hands: it's unreal for us.

Yet we should be doing something: helping in some way: Only in our love, our compassion & sharing their suffering can they become real; and us also!

2

My dear friends, you are in for a treat today   a short homily from me! But first a story, which if it's got a moral it escaped me. I saw it in the context of today's scriptures but for the life of me I can't see a real connection & I am still scratching my head !

THE PASTOR OF AN INNER-CITY PARISH, IS OUT FOR HIS AFTERNOON STROLL. HE SEES THIS TINY SKINNY KID 0N A DOORSTEP, JUMPING UP AND DOWN, TRYING TO RING

THE DOOR-BELL. THREE TIMES HE TRIES & THREE TIMES HE FAILS. So HE GOES UP AND SAYS, "LET ME HELP YOU, KID." So HE RINGS THE DOORBELL LOUD AND LONG. HE HEARS FOOTSTEPS WITHIN THE HOUSE AND HE SAYS TO THE KID, "WHAT DO WE DO NOW?" "WE GET TO HELL OUTA HERE FAST," SAYS THE KID, "THAT'S WHAT WE'LL DO." ALREADY DOWN ON THE STREET AND RUNNING FOR DEAR LIFE.

A friend was visiting the hospice chaplain. In the course of a conversation, the chaplain said that week, eight of the hospices' 30 patients had died. The visitor asked about the effect of so many deaths on the staff. That was tough , the chaplain said, and shared one particular story from the weekend. That Saturday, a woman who' d been there some months had a visit from her teenage son. It was a great visit, filled with laughs, fun & hugs . At noon, the boy said he was going to have lunch with friends but would be back later. But shortly after the mother called the nurse on duty, a lovely young woman, the patient ' s favorite. "I think this is it. I may be dying. " The nurse checked her vital signs and replied honestly , " It' s possible ! " The patient then asked the nurse, "Will you hold me? I think if you hold me, I'll do this well . " The nurse did not hesitate—she got in the bed & cradled that emaciated body & held her into eternity. The visitor asked the chaplain, "What about the nurse? What did it do to her?" He said the nurse had taken 4 days to go to the mountains to think & feel & decide whether to return .

"Do you think she 11 be back? The chaplain replied. "She will be back. You learn in a place like this that caring hurts—but when you really care you offer something special—and become special yourself. it mentions this statue —how people touch it, even kiss it, many with intensity & faith , but most by casual habit — a hint of harmless superstition! There' s another famous statue , this time of St. Peter in the Vatican, people have touched for 400 years. They say that if you touch it you' 11 return to Rome: it' s what I had in mind once when I touched it.

It occurred to me that "Touching" is a Catholic thing —in this narrow sense & in the broader sense of the use of body language, of the physical & intimate, in expressing faith . Desperation & faith informed the touch of this woman today & resulted in her healing & in Jesus singling her out to commend. I'm sure many others touched him in the narrow confines of the street, but her touch is different: it unleashes power from Jesus : just as was the faith of Jairus, the temple official whose little girl was so ill and whom Jesus touched in a life-giving way.

I think they' re a powerful challenge to meditate on our faith —how Christ touches us in all sorts of ways, in ways totally un—programmed & unprogrammable — as in these gospel stories — as well as our routine of liturgy & prayer of the Church, chiefly in the Eucharist & in the healing power of Penance It suggests no time is ordinary because its God' s time; and the power of God is in all time when we reach out to touch it in Faith.

Whether we regard ourselves as important folk like Jai just or forgotten, used, and cast aside like the woman who'd been helpless 12 long years, we'll have times of impotency ! Then we must heed Jesus" words to Jairus, his family, & 3 apostles, "Have faith & believe" . We pray today that these summer months our faith will be strong & our touch be sure and, all times but especially if we lose control , that we'll experience the powerful healing touch of the Lord like a woman & a little girl in the Galilee long ago; both helpless , both powerless in different ways , but in their powerlessness open to the saving power of the Lord Jesus.

3

12TH SUNDAY OF THE YEAR A 2005

First a word on Father's Day!

I'd thought the Greeting Card industry had a hand in it

to make a few fast bucks; but that's not so! "Father's Day" was first proposed by Mrs. John Dodd in 1909. She wanted a special day to honor her Dad, William Srnart, a civil war veteran, Widowed when his wife died in child-birth with their 6th child, he was left to raise the newborn his other 5 kids alone on a farm in Washington State, When she grew up, Mrs. Dodd realized her Dad's strength & selfless dedication in raising herself & her siblings as a single father, She figured they'd be many like her who'd want to honor their Dads. Father's Day was first observed in Spokane, Wash. June 19, 1910. In 1966 LßJ signed a presidential decree declaring the 3rd Sun of June Father's Day. So that's it! I didn't know this figure some of you are like me; and would like to know more! Today we salute all our fathers!

Now to the scriptures! Upon a first look at Jer. (RI), shadowy words jump out at one: whispering , denounce, trapped, "Vengeance, a tone the gospel picks up with words such as: secret, afraid, kill , destroy, denies, it's no coincidence that the Readings blend. The designers of the Lectionary intentionally pick RI with the gospel of the day in mind, guess then —certainly superficially— the overall tone of the readings is, what we we would call a real downer! One wonders and & asks, "Where's the Good News here?"

Then, after spending some time with the Readings, the overall impression that stuck with me could be summarized in a passage St. Theresa of Avila used as a bookmark: "Let nothing disturb you," it says, "Let nothing make you afraid: All things are passing! God never changes! Patience obtains all things; Nothing is lacking to the one who has God—God alone is enough!" The same is expressed in a popular hymn No 602 in our hymnal: Rob Dufford STS adaptation of Ez34 "Be not afraid!" we sing! go before you always. And I will give you rest."

A Journey Through Words

Jeremiah

God called ~~Jesus~~ to be a prophet in one of the most turbulent ages in the history of the Middle East, & in Israel of too. He saw the fall of one great empire (Assyria) the rise of a greater one (Babylon) & amid this turmoil, Israel, having been ruled by a succession of weak kings, contributes to her downfall by resisting this overwhelming force of history!

He was a Prophet for 40 years amid these political convulsions of the 7thC B.C: his interventions were many, and it was a thankless task! It was tough work being God's prophet then! He is threatened and then imprisoned many times: eventually he's exiled in Egypt. To top all that, he undergoes a crisis of faith! Sometimes he cries out, wondering why he, of all people, should've been chosen for this absurd mission. This find is all suggested in today's short passage!

The word "jeremiad" is in the dictionary, with roots in the prophet's frequent complaints to it means a prolonged lamentation or tale of woe! However—and the "however is noted well) the story of Jeremiah, the prophet, does not end here. His loyalty, and trust is unswerving & he gives himself to the Lord's Work whole-heartedly, even naively: to his prophetic role, even as events turn bitter and & he complains nonstop, which in a sense permits us to complain on the occasions when we're wading in rough, muddy waters! There's a great prayer of trust right here in first reading: The Lord, he

says, is with me like a mighty champion, then good Old fashioned it continues, over many persecutors I will not stumble, for they will not succeed. Then he goes on to praise Yahweh God, most profusely! On the Gospel — a few words! We have switched from Mark to Matt 10 here his missionary discourse in which he gathers together teachings of Jesus on the requirements of discipleship. The theme is the same as last week which is the selection of the 12 and the general vocation to follow Jesus. Specifically, here the Cost of Discipleship is stressed. Given the situation in Matthew's time it is totally realistic! His people have been through their Jeremiah experience — witnessing to Jesus was dangerous business! It led to hostility and division in families, and it was an age of confessors and martyrs. One could say things hadn't turned out as hoped, so in Matthew's gospel we have these frank & consoling words of Jesus for Matthew's church, for disciples in every age.

Persecution because of fidelity to Jesus will happen, but not a hair on their heads goes uncounted by God, not even a tiny sparrow goes unnoticed as it falls to ground, filling to the ground might suggest martyrdom! This is not faith: there will be moments of persecution, because we are to walk in the footsteps of Jesus —yet sprinkled though

scripture—3 times in the eight verses of the Gospel

alone —is the phrase "Be not afraid." I've read that it

occurs over 700 times in the Bible, and that is Good

News! What is the message for us? What we take

from it? We may not be in line to be witnesses &

martyrs of the caliber of Jer, *emiah* or the great moderns

like Oscar Romero, Dietrich ßonhoffer, or Martin

Luther King, or a litany of contemporary martyrs for

justice and peace, many of them unsung!

Yet fidelity in the Way, day in and day out

in little hidden things, daily, is demanding. We may

complain when the going is rough but that's ok—

We may feel overwhelmed, overridden &

insignificant in this loud secular age where a well-

known University can award an honorary PhD to

our arch—abortionist. When the pressure is big to

be born in this age of Howard Sterns, to be true to

Way of Jesus, it requires faith & trust — deep

trust— & we do it together! Each Sunday here we pick ourselves up and carry on!

A story from Nazi Germany to conclude!

Quite often evil times produce remarkable people of faith and courage; even when the great religious institutions which should be supportive then buckle beneath the pressure.! One such was Lutheran Pastor Martin Niemoller — not as famous as another pastor and martyr, Dietrich ßonhoffer, nonetheless a shining light in a dark age. Neimoller was on Adolf Hitler's most feared hated list, to silence him he was imprisoned. Months later he is summoned before a special court & suddenly he began to feel terribly afraid, not knowing what to expect.

He relates that as he was taken along a seemingly endless corridor from the prison cell to the courtroom, he heard a low voice. As he listened,

the voice quoted from the RC Latin Bible used then

in Germany. The Voice whispered a Verse from

Proverbs, which began: "Nomen Domini turris

fortissimo" the Lord's Name is a strong tower, the

righteous will run to it & and be strengthened safe Proverbs 18:10. It was the

jailer's voice - who it was is not known — but it had

an instant impact on Martin Nero where his fear

vanished and his confidence in God was renewed.

The invitation of Jesus is the same for all of us! It is

a call to radical discipleship, the antidote to our fears.

Before this call is radical trust as we journey, though

the going may be rough we may feel life is unfair!

For the gift to listen well to follow, for this Radical

Trust in Jesus' promises, we pray!

4

My dear friends, Scripture today suggests that we reflect for a little while on Hope. We've had the Journey of Hope recently which, if it did nothing else, helped in highlighting a virtue we didn't give the attention it deserved, and invited us to clarify what Christian Hope is; how essential it is for inner peace and fulfilment, and for a warm joyful human journey.

Firstly, I want to share with you another

parable, a reasonably contemporary one, which I think fits this theme well. It sheds light on the stories we've just listened to, in Ezekiel, and then in Mark's Gospel. The story I tell is true.

I found it in the introduction to a Missalette of three years ago I believe, the last time these readings came up. It struck me then how appropriate it was, and I tucked it away with my things for another time. It's about an eccentric Frenchman, named Elzeard Bouffier who turned a barren and colourless desert into a fertile land by planting trees - thousands of them!

It happened in the southeast of France, where he lived, where the Alps thrust into Provence. Once a lowland farmer, Bouffier lost his only child; and then his wife died. Alone, he withdrew to the mountains and became a shepherd. But he saw that the land, too, was near death from want of trees: so he began to plant. In the first 3 years, Bouffier planted 100,000 acorns. Twenty thousand sprouted, of which 10,000 were lost to rodents and climate.

But 10,000 oaks grew. He laboured, undaunted, unknown and unseen, except for the person who discovered him and wrote his story, returning to see the miracle he had performed. From 1910 to 1 947, ignoring two world wars, and D-day also, Bouffier planted oaks, lindens, beech, birch and maples, until one day a government official noticed with amazement that a "natural stand of forest" had sprung up in the wilderness. Streams long dry had begun to flow and willows grew again. Villagers and Hope returned together to the area. Even the harsh winds were tempered by the tall growth of trees. In the end, more than 10,000 people owed their prosperity to Elzeard Bouffier; and the planter himself, most of all, found his own fulfilment and happiness.

This true story of hills covered with forests is like the cedar, the mustard tree, and the seed sown by the farmer that grows mysteriously. All of them are Parables of the Kingdom of God, symbols of God's Fidelity and His Eternal Presence, of Resurrection and of Hope.

They are parables of silent power, of patience, of sacrifice, of trust in the unceasing activity of the Spirit accomplishing God's Will and building the Kingdom of God. These trees are living signs of life not just figuratively but in reality. The Tree of the Cross, planted on a high hill long ago, brought the Reign of God to earth. And that Tree is still growing today. We need to hear these stories often, to let them sink in for, despite all our progress, there is a great pessimism out there.

Ezekiel's prophecy belongs to the period of the Second Exile in Babylon. His people are oppressed and far from home; all the familiar comforting props are taken from them. The temple is destroyed, the great festivals and magnificent celebrations but a memory. Yet, even then, they are encouraged not to lose hope and to realize that their God is like a vigilant sleepless Watchman in the Night, caring for them. The Gospel also is encouragement for the early Church, and early Christian Communities facing a daunting task. A people persecuted and without earthly power, they are called to proclaim the Good News to a hostile Pagan World at the height of its power.

These Gospel stories are a sort of prophecy; because history tells how the Good News did spread; mainly among the poor, the powerless, the slaves; those who did not have the protection of powerful structures; who did not have political economic and military clout; and they didn't have the media on their side!

Precisely because of their lowliness, their humility,

their openness to the Spirit of Jesus, they're not being concerned with "human means" they were powerful instruments of the same Spirit. I think it is true to say that we appear to face an equally difficult world. There are powerful forces of darkness out there: and I say this not, I hope, in a fundamentalist "preachy" way. It may be that other times were as bad or worse than ours, but they didn't have TV to beam it into their households then, and brow beat them as it does us with its ugliness. At any rate, as I see it, my Faith doesn't appear to be as strong as it was; and Morality, as I thought I knew it tough, but objective and clearly defined that morality is challenged on all sides.

We tend to buy into and accept a chaotic moral relativism, and we bow down to an amoral political correctness. We are not at all so sure of the ground on which we stand any more. So, we tend to cry out in frustration, and we wring our hands in despair, because our way of thinking, our pet projects, are not working out as we would have them. We give in to the temptation to do it their way; a powerful temptation that even Jesus had to deal with and reject out of hand in the desert. Into this crisis, Christ speaks to us today. He invites us to trust, to be faithful in discipleship, to be patient and prayerful, to live in Hope that seeds sown in obscurity will bear fruit.

Archbishop Rembrandt Weakland of Milwaukee, in an article he wrote quite recently, said that we are called to live a New Asceticism, more challenging and trying than the old physical disciplines of Fasting and Penance; and I believe, more authentic: an asceticism of insecurity, uncertainty, and powerlessness, of not being in control. It means we must learn to let go, to root ourselves in the mystery of a surprising Christ, and His ever present and active Spirit. It means we learn to live in trust, and we learn to hope against hope. As the introduction in today's Missalette says:

"The Kingdom of God isn't our creation; it is pure gift of God who is Love. This kingdom is found in unexpected places; it thrives where love is stronger than indifference, where justice is stronger than greed, where truth is stronger. than power. The kingdom of God can't be controlled and manipulated: like quicksilver it escapes the grasp of the powerful and lives on among the simple. It is not meant to give prestige to the influential, but service to the poor and the powerless. "

We need to stand back, disengage, and realize these things: we possess a precious gift that no person or circumstance can take from us. There is an eternal dimension to our being that is rich and beautiful. The Lord's Day, and the Eucharist we celebrate together, is a great gift in so many ways; not the least being that it provides this opportunity, week by week, to relax and hand over our lives to the Lord Who never abandons us! And with Elzeard Bouffier, we keep planting trees!

5

The church air conditioning crashed so Vince the fixer, thought he'd check it out! He's up in the roof, and peeking down through a vent, sees an o neighbor kneeling at the statue of Mary, saying her Rosary. Vince is a joker; so, he calls out: 'hey Josie! This is Jesus & I've heard your prayer!" The old girl didn't blink an eye—she just kept on praying! so Vince calls out louder: "Josie, this is the Son of God: your prayer is answered!" Josie looks up & says, "be quiet, young man! I'm trying to talk to your mother!" It's a real oldie, but a pretty good one to get into our topic today: which is prayer!

It's clear in the first reading, Abraham haggling with God - like merchants in a Dutch flower market, or a Middle Eastern bazaar— is chosen as a backdrop to the Gospel to stress stubborn, almost annoying, perseverance in prayer and I'll leave it there! The second reading: the opening verse is a key to Christian prayer "You have received Christ Jesus, the Lord:" Paul says, "Continue then, to live your lives in Him, rooted and built up in him — full of thanksgiving." The Gospel is Luke's version of the Lord's prayer:

shorter than Matt & Mark, it's likely the closest to the words of Jesus. Matthew's version is closest to the one we rather use.

Here, Luke puts it in context — giving it as Jesus' reply to the disciples' "Lord," the disciples say: "Teach us to pray as John (the Baptist) taught his disciples." It would be instructive to know the kind of prayer "the wild man" John taught but we don't have it. one might talk about components of the Lord's prayer — taking care of God and taking care of our— selves - but it's my sense it would be redundant, and you'd be tempted to say — "get on with it"! simply remind myself when I say it, I'm close to Jesus' own prayer; and to the mind & heart of Jesus! After all, it's his own lived prayer & so it's a kind of window to his soul: it reveals his relationship with his "Abba" & it indicates his priorities. One writer says "The word "Abba" is a rare window into the consciousness of the historical Jesus, an unparallel way of talking to God.

People then didn't address God by this name. "The theologian, Joachim Jeremias says,

"Abba expresses the heart of Jesus' relationship to God. He spoke to God as a child to his father: confidently and securely, and yet at the same time reverently and obediently."

I'd like to share a few thoughts on my approach to prayer— such as it is! The Church's prayer, 'Liturgical prayer, we call it' is vital: it nourishes al prayer. but wish to ask what we do when we think we pray-& what it does to us! The dictionary sees prayer as a sort of begins asking for stuff—like Abraham, I guess! Successful prayer then is when you get the stuff, which is ok so far as it goes, but it's a limited thing! True prayer, as with Jesus is a conversation which aligns us with the Divine as one conceives this say in deference to other great traditions of prayer. It is surrender to the Mystery of God and the mystery of our own humanity under God, evoking heartfelt thanks, &

praise, & humility. The who other great prayers in Luke, Mary's 'Magnificat', and the prayer of Zachariah begin in praise & thanksgiving!

You may have heard —Tammy Faye Baker, the TV evangelist died recently of cancer: you will recall her— the lovely made-up partner of Jim baker! I find TV hard to take, & the Bakers especially hard! Then lately I heard her on Larry King when ravaged by cancer, down to 56 lbs.: in great pain! Asked how she handled it, she replied: "I accept: my faith helps." so, there is prayer & prayer: behind the TV image. Tammy Faye Baker was a woman of prayer. readily admit that, in my prejudice against religion I misjudged her.

Christian prayer is surrender to the Mystery of the God of Love we know in Jesus — we school ourselves in it by getting to know Jesus in his human-ness, letting him speak to us, being in his presence, seeing him in others, earning to trust Him! Words can interfere with prayer: Jesus said so!

What helps prayer along? A will and a desire to pray — scripture, especially the New Testament and the book of psalms, read to fuel the imagination for prayer: setting aside time for prayer —it need not be long — letting God in all the other times, so that it becomes a consistent prayer.

I like the Jesus Prayer— "Jesus, son of David, have mercy on me," it is scriptural & it simple, & has solid credentials especially in the world of OrthodoxChristianity, where they'll tell you fidelity to it has led to great holiness of life and made many saints! As a mantra, it helps make our days a prayer.

In our Tradition we try to keep the church open: we believe in Jesus' Presence and encourage you to drop in: We're open 9 to 9 Mon to Fri! Weekends are a bit problematic because of all the activity here, but you are always welcome. What to say —make your own formula prayers, the rosary & others you know: but don't let them get in the way!

I think nothing is often the best: simply be present & quiet & listening: being here, like Martha's sister, Mary, in last Sunday's Gospel!

To wrap this up! Joey, aged 6, asks his older sister a question! "Can anyone ever really see God?" Susie says, "Of course not, silly! God is so far you in heaven he can't be seen!" Later he asks Mom. "Not really," she says more gently. "God is spirit, he lives in our hearts, but we can't really see him!" Summer comes and he is on a fishing trip with granddad. They have a great time and catch a few fish also! One day, at sunset, Grandad leaves aside his fishing rod and he turns his full attention to a glorious sunset unfolding before them across the lake. Joey figures he may as well ask. So, he says: "Grandad, I wonder if anyone can really see God?" Grandad doesn't even turn his head. A long moment slips by before he replies. Then he says quietly: " Son, it's getting so I can't see anything else!" Maybe that's what we are aiming for. Amen!

6

A little story to start a Reflection.

There is a story about a lawyer who had a weak case to present in court. His client said to him, "You know, I have some nice fat geese at home. Would it help if I gave one to the Judge?" "Are you mad?" answered the lawyer, -"Don't know that this is the most upright, most righteous judge in the whole country?" They go into court and the presentation went even worse than expected. However, judgment was given in their favor and the lawyer is totally amazed. Later, the client said with a smile, "see how the goose worked!"-Don't tell me, said the lawyer, "that you sent the goose." The client replied, "I did -But sent it in the other fellow's name!"

There are many lessons from the Scriptures today: fun fact that sort of open—ended—ness is of the nature of parables! You don't find cut and dried dogma in the teaching of Jesus! One must settle on one or two lessons or else stay all day here! So simply I wish to draw your attention to two, which may be the two obvious ones.

First, going with my little story, there is an

inclination we have to meddle in other people's lives —
to put them down somehow to make ourselves look
better! Quite often we jump to wrong conclusions in
judging others who differ from us in so many ways —
like the righteous judge of that story — when we'd be
way better off much more in tune the kingdom — were
we out about trying to sow good seeds of compassion,
gentleness and generosity, and hospitality — & listening
our hearts as well as with our ears! we listen with the
heart we are nonjudgemental — and we become
receptive to the kingdom, to the seeds Jesus would sow
in us, to bear fruit in our lives. I'm thinking of the times
I've compared my Religion —or my expression of my
religion — to others or to other expressions of my
religion! I think of the times I've declared my school
better than the next school, my way of seeing things
way superior to the others way of seeing things!

I have another story to illustrate that — there
are very many stories because the issue is so basic! This

one speaks eloquently — a true story found it in the latest issue of "Connections." It's entitled, The Prison Angel" —the story of Mother Antonia. it's written dramatically, but you the bones of Born Mary Clark in LA, born to privilege, she was a great beauty in her time, neighbour of -Dinah Shore, Cary Grant; Twice married, she has 7 children who adore her. Her extensive charity work led to tension and divorce in her 2nd marriage, in 1977- her marriage over, her children grown, she wanted to do more. With her children's permission she sold her belongings drove to Tijuana, across the Mexican border from San Diego, where she had previously been making church sponsored relief visits, she became a nun. She is now 78 and for the past 28 years has lived in La Mesa, Tijuana's prison which houses 6000 dangerous inmates.

She lives there in residence: the only one of her community there- others work at rehabilitating ex-prisoners. Maru Clark is known and loved by the prison inmates and the prison staff all of whom refer to her as other Antonia. She's not the warden , nor a guard – simply Mothe Antonia, who spends the first hour of her day in prayer the, after many cups of coffee, spends 10 hours a day visiting prisoners, counselling the newly arrived, gong to the prison hospital-helping every way she can to alleviate their dreadful existence, doing all she can to simply be Christ to them- with loving care and without passing judgement she provides a listening ear. The warden says she's the most important person in the prison, "Mother Antonia," he says, "brings hope to the men and women here; and she finds hope in them." What drives her she says, is her faith: "My faith, is what makes my heart beat. Like a mother I always search for the best in my sons" No doubt Mother Antonia models the sower in our gospel, sowing seeds of encouragement and reconciliation, regardless of the hard prison "ground" on which is scattered; and ready and willing to do the hard work necessary to realize the harvest Jesus's promises.

But we don't have to be Mother Antonia's and we don't have to go to Tijuana to sow seeds of the Kingdom- we sow the seeds of the kingdom in ordinary every-day things, in the simple acts of kindness, patience, forgiveness, of hospitality, of non-judgemental love- a ready smile and warm embrace at home, at the office, in the store, on the road and most especially whem people truly annoy us. The humblest offers of help and affirmation are seeds bearing fruit for the glory of God, in His Kingdom- our God the sower of seeds in todays Gospel. It is not for us to worry about the outcome: our task is simply to be faithful and leave the outcome to God.

So we may never move far from Matthew Chapter 25- where the Lord of the kingdom says:

"Come, whom my father has blessed. I was hungry and you gave me food. I was thirsty and you gave me drink, I was naked and you clothed me, sick and in prison and you visited me. So the righteous will say "Lord, when did this happen?" then they'll hear in the answer: "As long as you did it to the least of these sisters and brothers of mine, you did it to me." This tells me God's kingdom is far bigger than our sometimes very narrow notion of Church!

7

A STORY, OR TWO, TO GET US

GOING!

HERE'S ONE THAT MIGHT EVEN BE TRUE! about Henry Ford, of the Ford Motor Corp: Ford was visiting the family ancestral village in Ireland.

Two trustees of a local hospital found out he was there & managed to get in to see him. They talked Ford into giving the 'hospital $5,000 (In the 1930's, five thousand was a great deal of money). Next morning, at breakfast, he opened his newspaper, to read the headline: "American Millionaire Gives $50,000 to Local Hospital."

Ford immediately summoned the two trustees. Waving the newspaper in their face, he demanded. "What does this mean?" The trustees apologized profusely. "A big mistake, sir" they said. They promised a retraction the very next day, declaring that the great Henry Ford had given, not fifty thousand, but only five. Hearing this, Ford offered them another forty-five thousand, under one condition: the trustees would erect a marble arch at the new hospital entrance, and place upon it a plaque that read, "l walked among you, a native son, & you took me in!"

STORY NUMBER 2 IS DIFFERENT BUT DOES HAVE BEARING ON WHAT I WANT TO SAY.

A teacher, trying to explain to a class of small children what "'faith" is, told the story of young Peter on a sailing vessel. The pet monkey snatches his cap and darts up into the rigging: Pete climbs up after him, higher and higher into the rigging, he goes, till the sailors are horrified as they see him showing signs of dizziness & about to fall headlong to the deck. Afraid to climb up to rescue him, his dad shouts up: "Jump out into the water and we'll catch you" Pete hesitates a moment and then, trusting his father's wisdom, make a great leap, and is pulled from the waves... not a bad description of the Leap of Faith that is grounded in Love. And Trust.

IT HAPPENS OFTEN, I THINK, WHEN WE TRY TO INTERPRET THE TEACHING OF JESUS. FOR A VARIETY OF REASONS, ALL VERY HUMAN: WE VEER OFF-COURSE FROM THE MESSAGE. THE OBVIOUS TODAY IS WHEN THIS SCRIPTURE IS USED.

There are many stories like this poking fun at a serious matter - just as serious today as in Moses's day when Joshua complained to Moses about Eldad & Medad and urged that he put a stop to their prophetic work. We find it too among the early Christians, whose churches were not nearly as cohesive as ours, and where clearly some figured themselves to be the insiders with power while excluding others. I certainly think this narrowness is at the heart of the Readings certainly first reading and the Gospel which complement each other as they so often do. It's the

Question of bigotry and jealousy, and whether one person or group has exclusive access to God -who's right & wrong in the matter of religion. Fr Munachi Ezeogwu tells a tale from Nigeria illustrating it well.

A priest - a holy man no doubt & an organizer! begins a high-profile prayer ministry in the pastoral center. There are others in the Diocese but none as big as his, now this man goes to the bishop & has him sign a decree that his is the only one recognized - so anyone needing the healing ministry in the diocese must go only to his center. What the document says, in effect, is God has no right to heal anybody except at the pastoral center!

This temptation to restrict God's reach, and to control God, is alive & well and is especially strong in groups that demand total loyalty - loyalty was immensely important to groups such as that which formed round Jesus - and their reaction to the stranger who casts out demons seemingly without authority stems from that misplaced loyalty. I think it's a trend that's beginning to surface in our Catholic Church again, despite the openness of the teaching of the second Vatican Council.- Reginald Fuller commenting on these very readings cautions against "clerical arrogance that refuses to recognize the charisms possessed by members of the church." In more pessimistic moments, I sense in some circles a return to harsh & rigid clericalism.

- an attempt to curb freedom of expression, restricting a laity who've known some freedom & respect certainly in the 40 years since I got into this business! It's a pharisaic rigidity which seems foreign to how Jesus acts & speaks today & in the Gospels time & again. I think that fidelity to Jesus involves our combating this rigid legalism by our lives of openness and generosity and respect for every person - never forgetting the cup of cold water which brings divine approval whoever serves it. I feel we do just that very well here in d'Youville, and its why I love the parish and pray we keep it so. For me today's Word of God is a challenge

"I HAD A GOOD GAME OF TENNIS BACK THEN."

8

A lady is having a hairdo before traveling to Rome with her husband: she's all excited since it's her first trip over—seas. "Rome!" says her hairdresser. "Why would you go there? It's crowded, dirty, stinking hot this time of year, & full of loud Italians! So, how you getting there?" "We fly Al Italia," she says. "That's a horrid airline," says he. "Their planes are old &

dangerous, the flight attendants ugly, and they' re

always late. So, where you stay? " "An exclusive little

place on the West Bank of the Tiber —Parco —"Say

no more, says the hairdresser. "I've stayed there once ;

it' s awful, rotten service, musty , old, no air—

conditioning, over—priced. So what you doing there?"

"We' re going to the Vatican & we hope to see the

Pope" . "That's rich, " he laughs, "you & a million

others trying to see him. He'll be a mile away and he'll

look the size of an ant —Good look any way: you'll be

needing it." A month later she comes in again for a

hairdo. The hairdresser asks about her trip to Rome."

Fabulous , she says. " Not only did we get there on

time, we're on a splendid new Airbus : and they

bumped us up to 1st class: the steward was the

handsomest young man I ever saw & the food was out

of the world. And my! The hotel: it was splendid: they'

d just finished a $10m renovation job on it: it' s the

jewel of Rome —the finest in the city. Since they' d over—booked too they gave us the royal suite at no extra cost." "That' s all well & good, " mutters the hairdresser, "but I know you didn't get to see the Pope . "Actually, we did, " she says." An amazing thing happened. As we toured Vatican, this Swiss Guard taps my husband on the shoulder: tells us the Pope likes to see some visitors to St. Peter's, if we'd be so kind as step into his private room the Pope would personally greet us. Sure enough, 5 minutes later, in comes John Paul II in the flesh. I almost fainted, she said." He shook my hand as I knelt down & spoke to me " "Really," says the hairdresser," and what did he say?" He said, "Oh my God! Where did you get that lousy hairdo?"

So, you ask, how I justify that one ! I guess, I could say, its vacation season, & marvelous things happen if we' re open & attentive. Indeed, good things happen even if it' s not right now: so long as we' re tuned in & aware we live in God' s beautiful world.

Most likely we'll not see the Pope this Summer, but the Lord comes & goes in our lives all the time: and we are invited to be tuned in, receptive to His Comings . We have the example of Abraham' s exquisite hospitality and courtesy in welcoming the 3 strangers who arrive on his doorstep, & who turn out to be divine messengers with the most wonderful news imaginable for himself and his wife, Sarah. Then of course there the story of Mary of Bethany today: Mary in the Gospel , attentively listening to the Master , while Martha her sister anxiously fusses & complains about her sister ,it's a lovely story and deceptive in it' s simplicity: one could spend a lot of time analyzing it, but I won' t: It' s often quoted to stress the importance of prayer & living in the presence of God. Jesus was close to the 2 sisters & their brother Lazarus: it' s likely he stayed with them when he was in Jerusalem, because it was only 3km, or so, from the Temple, and it was on the route he' d follow, along the Jordan valley from the Galilee, via Jericho.

Fr Andrew Greeley, author of some steamy novels, who likes to shock , says the two girls were in love with Jesus, which is possible, but we Catholics are suspicious of romantic love, even though we admit he was a man, and even an attractive man: and we don' t dwell on it. Later, the final days , we learn from John that Mary poured precious perfume on Jesus body to Judas Iscariot' s huge chagrin, then washed his feet & dried them with her hair. Such an act of intimacy would suggest a deep level of human love: Mary' s an unconventional girl ! she does unexpected things ; The rabbis would be horrified; they wouldn't' t dare allow a woman to sit for teaching Martha' s strong too . She can hold her own with anybody, Jesus' love & respect for her is quite obvious: here & certainly in the other places she' s mentioned. I think Jesus ' reply is somewhat like his answer to his mother on one occasion: He' s so in tune with her, so comfortable in her home, that he can say what' s on his mind without mincing words . That' s an important part of hospitality, & deep friendship & discipleship & a readiness to grow , & we can all learn!

They stand out, the two of them, in a male world; there' s plenty of room for a feminist kind of homily, and it's tempting to dwell on it, Mary' s intent listening is commended by Jesus while Martha is rebuked in a loving way, not because she' s hospitable but because she fusses too much and is distracted. But she' s not afraid to talk strong to Jesus , even though she' s a woman. Fr. Jude Siciliano has a neat commentary on this gospel story, seeing a connection with the early house churches in the word used for serving , DIAKONIA , from which we get the office of deacon. The only churches then were house churches , like one preserved in Capharnaum today, that tradition says was in Peter' s home. He says that in the early days the apostolic group would travel about much the same as Jesus did with his disciples . The women would look after their needs & serve them, as they did for Jesus. But then , is that all they should do? Are they to be relegated to the role of servants only, with no right to active membership, to hear & to teach? He suggests this story addresses this issue; and that strong women like Mary & Martha took a stand then & insisted on their rightful place; against a culture that kept them in the kitchen only: as it still tends to do in the Moslem world, and indeed in our world too, unless the Marys' & Marathas" insist on their rightful place: interesting stuff but I've said enough.

Fr. Siciliano concludes his piece suggesting we dwell on the importance of grounding all activity in prayer and living non—stop in the presence of God. He has some examples, his mother included. I'm a strong believer in the style of prayer as a way of underpinning my activity —such as it is—with prayer: I even try to practice it. It' s a type of prayer associated

with Asian tradition, but it' s got deep Christian Roots.

John Cassian, a great teacher of spirituality in the 5th

century, taught his monks this prayer & St. Benedict

learned from him, and passed it on to his monks. We

take a phrase or a word of scripture & repeat it on our

lips, then in our hearts 'til it becomes part of us . The

Jesus Prayer is very popular in the Orthodox tradition .

"Jesus, Son of David, have mercy on me ." They say

many a simple monk reached a high level of union with

God, by saying & internalizing that prayer: saying it as

they worked on the monastery farm, in the workshop

or scriptorium , till it became part of them. Two words,

Aramaic words, the language Jesus spoke, I like are

"Abba" —the Aramaic for Father— because Jesus

used it meaning " Poppa/Momma, the most intimate

word one could use to address a parent. Jesus used the

word "ABBA" to address his heavenly Father.

"Maranatha" means "Come , Lord Jesus" It's the last

word of the New Testament, & of Rev & the Letter to the Corinthians . It too is Aramaic and there' s good reason to believe it was on the lips of Christians in apostolic times. For me they are simply connecting words & this prayer the most meaningful & do-able kind. Somehow it keeps me in the Mary Mode and makes my life a prayer .

9

If we had a billboard outside, as Protestant Churches do, the title Of this Homily of mine would be the Ordinariness of the Kingdom!" The Gospel consists of 3 short parables of Jesus — a hidden Treasure, a Priceless Pearl, a Net east in the sea, which is a double, a story of divine patience, similar to last week's Parable of the Weeds! So, guess I'm entitled to 3 stories which have a native shrewdness — a wisdom akin to the Hebrew wisdom Solomon prays for gets,The 1st is about an expensive donkey Frankie, a city boy is out in the country one day and he buys the donkey from farmer Bob for $200. Bob agrees to deliver it next day. But next day, he drives up says, "sorry, I've got bad news: the donkey died." well, says Frankie, give me back my money!" can't do says Bob, with a grin, says something significant about parables of the kingdom* They're not moral stories about what's right & wrong they simply point to the kingdom — here today asking how ready we are to give up everything for the kingdom's sake. Jesus tells stories, from where he is — and where his listeners are, homespun stories that point to the kingdom as the summum bonum, the supreme good that has a Value worth pursuing at any cost. But the company Jesus moves in isn't always kosher! He consorts with tax collectors, with prostitutes — & a rag tag band of disciples. He associates with the polloi and appears to avoid the rich and famous, so annoying the Pharisees no end! love is the great Messiah Himself, the Son of God, Jesus, announcing his father s Kingdom, come to proclaim justice truth love yet in a real world, an imperfect world, and he knows it: and his stories reflect it! They've got an earthiness there is absolutely no need to justify —no humbug whatsoever!

He tells us we are children of the kingdom, God's chosen, beloved, though we are imperfect, vessels of clay! We sprout all sorts of weeds in our own which hopefully keeps us humble; and we function in an imperfect world and we mustn't be overwhelmed by it, as Jesus we're to go about building the kingdom in our milieu, We try to make the Reign of God recognize and we do so in a real world to which we belong — & we do it with 100 % dedication, generosity, and compassion, and with no thought of reward, because it's the Way of Jesus: it's the priceless Pearl, the ultimate Treasure!

Some writers recently have pointed to disillusionment of young Muslims with a coarse and corrupt secular word as reason for their radicalization. While we abhor and denounce the terrorism that it may have caused, we can sympathize with them — frustrated as we may be with a cultural elimination where, the name of freedom of speech "and a secular of Rights" says bestially anything goes — there is no moral law, no rules, no private morality — there is no (order in the universe, no kingdom of)— there is an inclination for us to fight back!

Like Jesus, who operated an imperfect world, the Gecko—Roman world of the we followers, who try to walk in his way and his truth — we fight back, as it were, by announcing the Kingdom of God especially following our living with composure and compassion — and with a tolerance of -points of view and lifestyles different from ours — a tolerance rooted in love for humanity. We do it also because we are confident that the Reign of God will win, ultimately!

The question as I see it is this: to what extent do we buy into the kingdom of Jesus? I think many of us buy into the extent that it doesn't interfere too much with our lifestyles! One writer expresses it this way: I like to buy worth of God, please — not enough to explode my soul or disturb my sleep —what will equal a cup of warm milk or a snooze in the sun! don't want enough of God to make me love a homeless man or to pick berries with a migrant worker — just a little ecstasy will do, not transformation — the warmth of the womb, not a new birth! I want the Eternal in a sack, like to buy 5 dollars' worth of God, please.

Today's Parable of the Treasure Pearl challenges us to ask why we settle so readily for five dollars' worth, How much is our worth? Of what value is a sense of the presence of God, of a simple Christ centered lifestyle of the peace meaning such realities can bring into one's life? Today's parables say that such a lifestyle is the supreme value, and worth everything.

Just one more story I think apropos! A wise man reaches the outskirts of a village, He settles down under a tree for the night when a man came running up to him and said, "The stone! stone! Give me the precious stone!" What stone?" asks the wise man, The poor man said, "Last night the Lord appeared to me in a dream, and he told me that he went to the outskirts of the Village at dusk to find a wise man who'd give me a precious stone that would make me rich forever." The wise man rummaged in his bag and pulled out a stone. I guess he meant this one, he said as he handed him the stone, he found it on a forest path some days ago, you can certainly have it. The man looks at it in wonder. it was a magnificent diamond: the largest in the world, large as a man's head! He took it from the wise man and walked away. That night the poor man tossed about in bed, unable to sleep, Next day at the crack of dawn he woke the wise man and said: "Here: take your diamond! Give me, rather, the wealth that makes it possible for you to give this diamond away so easily." Lord, grant us such wisdom!

10

God is alive and well and is especially strong in groups that demand total loyalty - loyalty was immensely important to groups such as that which formed round Jesus - and their reaction to the stranger who casts out demons seemingly without authority stems from that misplaced loyalty. I think it's a trend that's beginning to surface in our Catholic Church again, despite the openness of the teaching of the second Vatican Council.- Reginald Fuller commenting on these very readings cautions against "clerical arrogance that refuses to recognize the charisms possessed by members of the church." In more pessimistic moments, I sense in some circles a return to harsh and rigid clericalism.

- an attempt to curb freedom of expression, restricting a laity who've known some freedom & respect certainly in the 40 years since I got into this business!

It's a pharisaic rigidity which seems foreign to how Jesus acts and speaks today & in the Gospels time & again. I think that fidelity to Jesus involves our combating this rigid legalism by our lives of openness and generosity and respect for every person - never forgetting the cup of cold water which brings divine approval whoever serves it. I feel we do just that very well here in d'Youville, and its why I love the parish and pray we keep it so. For me today's Word of God is a challenge to remain faithful -while careful to deepen our own faith in prayer and action for the Kingdom, we must never put down others; nor consider ourselves superior to them. It's call to humility in our own faith and hospitality & respect in our dealings with other traditions, & others in our tradition, who think and act differently to us. I think Jesus was pretty upset with John & the others, their narrowness, bigotry, and exclusivity -it led him to this outburst about cutting off hands & stuff, to utter such hard words. I remember well one of the most difficult things I had dealt with in this community even though it's got to be nearly 20 years ago. I got a call one Saturday morning in Jan or Feb, a cold morning with snow on the ground ... a young man found dead on his doorstep. I knew him - he was bright but a bit off center, heavy into the bible and into drugs also. We tried to help but this night he found a butcher's knife and cut off his right hand at the wrist. When the police checked they found this scripture underlined in the bible in his room. Clearly it would be ridiculous to think this was what Jesus mean but there are those who could and have used these texts as a cudgel to clobber people over the head with.

12

You know I was in NFLD this past summer and I loved it! There's his   little story that's got a NFLD flavor that I'll begin with. A backslider Begins attending Mass faithfully Sunday mornings instead of going fishing. Delighted, the pastor said, "It's wonderful to see you back with us at Mass again with your good wife!" "Well, Rev," says the fisherman, "it's a matter of choice. I'd rather hear your sermon than hers."

Anthony De Mello has a story you may've

heard. In Belfast, a Priest, Minister, and Rabbi are engaged in a heated argument. From nowhere an angel appears and says, "God sends you, His blessings. "You each make one wish for peace & your wish will be granted." The minister says, "Let every Catholic disappear from our lovely island: then peace will reign." The priest says, "Let there not be a single protestant left on our Irish soil: that will bring peace to this island." "And what about you, Rabbi?" asks the angel. "Do you have no wish of your own?" "No," says the rabbi. "Just attend to the wishes of these two gentlemen and I shall be well pleased!" I place it in its context here and in the context of literature of the time where exaggeration was a technique to emphasize strongly - here a warning against bigotry, narrowness, exclusivity, playing God. We do well, when we feel like being critical and controlling, to remember all the beautiful stories where Jesus, in his love, reached out to those who were considered untouchable - to lepers, prostitutes, and Samaritans, to strangers and sinners of every stripe - and even to women! - without discrimination.

For the grace to be joyful and at peace, to be grateful for every manifestation of compassionate love, of prayer and spirituality in people, and in systems we don't particularly like, while being faithful to our own revelation, I pray this be the grist for the mill of our prayer today.

The headline news is of course the Passing of Pierre Eliot Trudeau , our former PM — a great Canadian, a person I admired intensely. He died yesterday round 3pm in Montreal . I have never been a lover of politicians, but I liked everything about the man, his intelligence, his flair, his vision, his loyalty to this country under great pressure, his touch and great love for his family, his commitment to a just & peaceful society for every person at home and internationally.

Many would say the death of his son, Michel, who was swept away in an avalanche while skiing in BC two years ago was more than he could take; he just didn't have the will any more to fight the diseases that plagued him Parkinson' s & Prostrate Cancer. There will be a lot about him in the media over the next few days and I encourage everyone to follow the events closely. We will be marking the passing of a great Canadian; maybe the greatest — a man known and admired across the world.

Brian McKenna, who with his brother, made a documentary on Trudeau' s life that will be played and replayed. Brian McKenna knew him well, respected him, and quoted poet, Stephen Spender, saying snatches of the poem just kept ringing in his head ever since he heard of Pierre Eliot Trudeau' s Death. It' s a beautiful poem, one I love, and I share it with you, you'11 pick up on the core message, I'm sure.

The Truly Great
BY STEPHEN SPENDER

I think continually of those who were truly great.

Who, from the womb, remembered the soul's history.

Through corridors of light, where the hours are suns,

Endless and singing. Whose lovely ambition

Was that their lips, still touched with fire,

Should tell of the Spirit, clothed from head to foot in song.

And who hoarded from the Spring branches?

The desires falling across their bodies like blossoms.

What is precious, is never to forget

The essential delight of the blood drawn from ageless springs

Breaking through rocks in worlds before our earth.

Never to deny its pleasure in the morning simple light

Nor its grave evening demand for love.

Never to allow gradually the traffic to smother

With noise and fog, the flowering of the spirit.

Near the snow, near the sun, in the highest fields,

See how these names are fêted by the waving grass!

And by the streamers of white cloud

And whispers of wind in the listening sky.

The names of those who in their lives fought for life,

Who wore at their hearts the fire's Centre.

Born of the sun, they travelled a short while toward the sun.

And left the vivid air signed with their honour

13

I've read a lot of stories that try to throw light

on this rather difficult gospel . I'11 share two of them with you :

An angel appears at a parish council meeting and tells the Pastor that he has come to reward him for his years of devoted service. So, he was asked to choose between three blessings: infinite wealth, infinite fame, or infinite wisdom! Without hesitating the Rev. asks for infinite wisdom. "You got it" says the angel and with that he disappears . All heads turn towards the pastor who sits glowing in the aura of wisdom. Finally, the chairman whispers to him, "Say something," he says the priest looks at them and says, "I should have taken the money."

Now for story number 2! Fr. Mark Link has it and tells it in this context. Some time ago a priest was giving a retreat to inmates of a federal prison in a Southern State. One of his talks was about Jesus's teaching on revenge you'11 recall, "You have heard that it was said, 'An eye for an eye and a tooth for a tooth. '

But I say to you, 'offer no resistance to one who is evil .

When someone strikes you on the right cheek, turn and

offer him the left" I can't but think of those terrorists

that the world community so desperately want to track

down: the planning, the cunning and pure brilliance of a

plan conceived and followed through on, all the

sacrifices made to do that evil deed . The "world" in the

Gospels is being equated with what draws us down and

away from compassion & forgiveness , away from the

God of Love. But I think also of Pope John Paul, old

and feeble, now in Kazakhstan, his 95th trip outside

Italy and possibly the most dangerous. Here is our

leader, totally devoted to the kingdom, using all means

at his disposal , going to every corner of the world, to

proclaim a gospel of peace and justice, and human

solidarity against evil. And I think of myself and my

compromises, my ambivalence in proclaiming the

Good News, and I pray for the grace to be moved by

this most challenging of scriptures: moved to be more

faithful.

You may've heard this one, or a variation on it!

People called BRIDIE a saint for her patience with her husband: she died & arrived at the Gates of Heaven. As she waited for St. Peter to greet her, she peeked Through the Gates. She saw inside a banquet table and sitting around if her parents and all the others she'd loved and who had gone before her. When Peter came by, she said, "This place is fantastic, amazing! How do I get in?" "You'll have to spell a word," St. Peter told her. "Which word?" the woman asked. "LOVE," Peter said. She spelled "LOVE" and St. Peter welcomed her into heaven. Six months later Peter came and asked her to watch The Gates of Heaven for him that day. While she was on duty, guarding the Gates, her husband arrived. "I'm surprised to see you here," says Bridie, "How have you been? "Oh!

I've been doing pretty well since you died," he told

her. "I married that beautiful nurse who took care of you while you were ill. Then we won the lottery. We sold the little house you and I lived in and bought a mansion. Then my wife and I traveled around the world. We were on vacation and went water skiing Today. I fell, the ski hit my head and here I am." Then he demanded, "So, how do I get in?" "You will have to spell a word," Bridie she him. "Which word?" he asked. She replied, "phantasmagoria."

A few days ago, the 28th, we had the feast of the saints, Simon & Jude, apostles. Almost nothing is known of them except they are among the twelve Jesus chose, and the Gospels are careful that we not confuse them with Simon Peter on the one hand, & Judas the betrayer, on the other: there's some obscure legends. They could be patrons of all anonymous people. In this vein, I found a quote which won't so away; I think appropriate to this feast of All Saints: Pope John Paul II, himself officially canonized, declared almost 500 people sainted: given enough time I might be able to name ten of them - no more! Me: I am thinking of ordinary people who are saints with no name: many I knew in this community!

This is the passage: Their egos left no trace - like a flight of birds in the sky. They are the patrons of the vast majority of Christians, of the saints, all who've ever lived. There is a lot to be said for silence and anonymity: they can give depth. Without Simon and Jude, the New Testament would be poorer: it would be all light and little shade. We might not so easily see ourselves in it.

Now a little history: the story of the stained-glass window in Winchester Cathedral. During the 17thC conflicts following the Reformation in England, Protestant Roundheads - a name given to Parliamentary Troops under Oliver Cromwell - then at war with the Royalists - they stormed into churches to destroy the religious symbols which they took to be idols. When they came to great medieval cathedral of Winchester, they shattered a huge stained-glass window which had long been a defining symbol of that church, dominating it with its beauty. When The Roundheads had finished, fragments of the brilliantly colored glass lay all over the stone floor. Those shards of glass, stunning Rembrandt-like depictions of biblical stories were so thoroughly broken that they could never be restored to form the original picture.

So, the congregation faced the Question -what to do: to throw out the glass and board up the window seemed the obvious solution: but it's not what they did. Instead, after the Restoration they lovingly gathered up all the pieces of glass & re-leaded them into a wonderful colorful design - long before the concept of abstract art was developed. Today, 300 years later, that window breaks the sunlight into a kaleidoscope of colors that splash down onto the church below, creating beauty and wonder out of an experience that was senseless and tragic.

I like to check my stories: I found this on Wikipedia! "The cathedral's huge mediaeval stained glass West Window was deliberately smashed by Cromwell's forces following the outbreak of the Civil War in 1642. After the restoration of the monarchy in 1660, the broken glass was gathered up & assembled randomly, in a manner something like pique assiette mosaic work- a mosaic made from broken pieces of an original. There was no attempt to reconstruct the original. Out of necessity, the cathedral pre-empted collage art by hundreds of years: you can see a photo of the window and the interior of the Cathedral: it has the longest Gothic Centre aisle of any Cathedral in England, so there you have it!

I think if the story of the shattered window is a lovely metaphor for the Christian life! God, in his amazing love takes all we're going through, our frayed bruised humanness - the good and bad, and indifferent, and creates something new and beautiful from it: it is what we call GRACE - the Work of the spirit. Speaking of Stained Glass! You may've noticed, looking closely at our windows, that today's Gospel the 8 Beatitudes - are inscribed, one at the bottom of each window - with a few other biblical quotes suggesting we are more interested in the here than the hereafter! This Gospel which marks the beginning of the Sermon on the Mount, gives us the distilled essence of the Way to Heaven! Jesus is the new Moses proclaiming His Way: it's his Manifesto. As children home in Ireland we had to memorize it - we had to memorize a lot stuff back then! I suggest that we all should, then we try to live it - first of all detachment.

- 'Blessed the Poor in spirit" - in the positive sense of living in the freedom of the children of the kingdom: then gentleness, compassion, the pursuit of justice and peace - and so on! That is the agenda for us!

However, to be a saint - there are many among us and I believe very many surprises - to be a saint, is above all a work of God, a work of grace, of the Spirit, on our bruised and wayward humanness: as it was with the twelve chosen ones. As we share the lessons, we've learned from what others teach us, God forms our lives into a dazzling display of the kingdom of heaven on earth: a kaleidoscope of lives, of shared faith, backward & forward in time, shining with the love of Christ. We may be saints with broken halos, but we're part of a grand design, going about our lives, filling this dark world with love and joy.

14

Wisdom from George Bush: "You've heard it said: "if someone strikes you on the right cheek, turn to him the other also," but I say unto you: "if someone even looks like they might have the ability to strike, nuke 'em! " Submitted by STK. The Pope was travelling by limousine to an appointment in Dallas. The Pope kept trying to hurry the driver. Frustrated and running late, He insisted that they trade places. The Pope sped down the freeway in the limo far exceeding the speed limit. A police officer pulled him over and called in to his chief " I don't know WHO is in the back of the limousine, ... but THE POPE is driving for him! " No ticket was issued. P. Gossett.

God summons Boris Yeltsin, Bill Clinton, and Bill Gates to a meeting. At the meeting he told them he was coming again, and the end of the world was next week. Go back and prepare.

Boris Yeltsin summoned his parliament and told them he had two things to tell them, and both were bad news. 1. There is a God. 2. The end of the world is next week.

Bill Clinton went back and summoned the Senate and said I have good news and bad news. 1. There is a God 2. the end of the world is next week.

Bill Gates went back and called his board meeting and said I have two items of good news.

1 . I am one of the three most important men in the world. 2. There is no millennium bug problem.

Hillary Clinton died and went to heaven. St. Peter met her at the gate and ushered her in. Hillary looked around and saw clocks everywhere. She said to St. Peter "Why are all these clocks here?" St. Peter replied, "Hilary, every time someone on earth told a lie, one second moved on the clock." Hillary looked around and saw one clock that had not "ticked off' one second. She asked, "Whose clock is that?" St. Peter replied, "That's Mother Teresa's clock. She never told a lie in her life." "That's wonderful, " Hilary replied. She looked at another clock and it appeared two seconds had "ticked off " Whose clock is that? Hilary inquired. "That's Abraham Lincoln's clock" St. Peter replied. "He only told two lies in his life." That's amazing! Hillary replied. She then asked St. Peter "Where's Bill's clock, Peter?" "Oh, it's upstairs" Peter replied. "Jesus is using it as a ceiling fan!"

If you get an envelope from a company called the "Internal Revenue Service," DO NOT OPEN IT!

This group operates a scam around this time every year. Their letter claims that you owe them money, which they will take and use to pay for the operation of essential functions of the United States government. This is untrue! The money the IRS collects is used to fund various inefficient and pointless social engineering projects. This organization has ties to another shady outfit called the Social Security Administration, who claim to take money from your regular paychecks and save it for your retirement. In truth, the Social Security Administration uses the money to pay for the same misguided make-work projects the IRS helps mastermind. These scam artists have billed honest, hard-working Americans out of billions of dollars. Don't be among them! Please copy this envelope in triplicate according to the guidelines of the "Paperwork Augmentation Act" of 1999 and then tear up all three of these envelopes a hundred pieces and send the pieces to the following address: IRS,

"FORM 1040 - NOT EZ" - Rejected Refunds

Division Office 1600, Room 412, Cubicle 13, Desk7,

Filing Cabinet 6, Drawer 3, space 62, Folder 5

Washington, DC 20000-0000

The special moments we never forget: some sad, others joyful.

I remember the exact moment of President 'John 'F Kennedy's Assassination: I was in the Seminary then and we were not supposed to have radios: so, the Dean calls us down to break the -news - it was about 5 in the afternoon! Of course, there were -radios I being a good seminarian didn't have one! So the word was already out, whispered along the corridors: we knew, soon as the news was out: there was some dissembling but the 'dean was shrewd- He knew: now he did! 'It is stiff so very clear in my mind.

We all have special moments in time -

mostly intimate that won't go away. So, John, assembling his gospel many years later knew even then the exact moment when they went and saw the place where Jesus stayed: and from then on, they abide with him, going wherever he goes, listening attentively to him, trusting him, absorbing his teaching, modeling their lives on his! I think there's Message here for us which is of —real value and worthwhile as we set out into this New Year of grace.

My friend acts towards people while most of us tend to 'react'! My friend has a sense of inner balance which is lacking in most. He knows what he stands for, how to behave. He refuses to return incivility for incivility, for he would then no longer be in charge of his own conduct. It's an 'inner balance' we recognize in John the Baptist! Coming from his knowing who Jesus truly is it enabled him to let go of his own dreams so that Christ would take center stage. or me, it's an inner balance Pope Benedict would have us find for ourselves. His Encyclical Letter is written is simply as a meditation designed to create in us a stillness & a composure; a hopefilled joy way of living in the midst of our crazy and loud world. It's an inner balance that we hope and pray for today. It brings peace: & it makes Christ and his Church attractive when we testify to Him in this very genuine man and Catholic Way! Amen

We have here ow we've come to know Jesus and like Benedict, have learned to put our faith and hope in him. Let me share a story of one man's Christian witness! It's told by Sydney Harris about a friend! He writes! I walked with my friend, a Quaker, to the newsstand the other night where he bought a paper, thanking the vendor politely." The man ignored him. Rude fellow isn't he', said. "Oh, he's that way every night," shrugged my friend. "Then why do you continue to be polite to him", I asked. My friend replied, "And why not! Why should I let him decide how I'm going to act? Harris then observed: "As he thought about this incident, it occurred to me that the important word. disciples began to believe in him.": "the first manifestation that, in Jesus, is God's residing glory!"

These testimonies can confuse one who has only read Mark, where disciples come to faith-knowledge of Jesus only hesitantly, timidly, & imperfectly and over a long period of time. John seems to contradict Mark since his disciples appear to know all there is to know about Jesus, even his divinity. We must realize that John is not attempting to give a historical presentation of the first disciples' growth in faith. He simply wishes to impress these statements about Jesus on the minds of his audience at the start. In a series of manifestations, we are given the required information. They show the main interest of the Gospel IS who this man Jesus is — what they call Christology!

The Second Sunday: Year A: 2008

In the Northern Portuguese town of Sobrado, a dog named Preta — Blackie! leaves her owner's home Sunday morning at 5 & walks 16 miles in time to take her usual place next to the altar for Mass. The dog stands and sits when the congregation does. She usually walks home, though parishioners give her a ride on occasions. A paper there has reported that church attendance has grown dramatically since word about the dog has gotten out. I guess one could give a whole homily on that story but I simply mention it to reflect a little on testifying, which is big in these scriptures: but first a diversion of sorts, though it might be seen as a kind of witnessing!

I have read Pope Benedict latest Letter on Hope you can download it from the Internet— it's on my mind as I share my thoughts with you! It's a meditation on a life of Faith, with deep roots in scripture but finely.

when as a young man he heard a voice but didn't recognize it because Israel then had forgotten the Covenant and abandoned her God! After much prompting Samuel recognizes that it is the Lord speaking to him & so he replies, "ere am ord" ready to do as you would have me do. I think it would be an excellent morning prayer for us disciples; to be on our lips and in our hearts all times!

The Gospel is John's account of Jesus' baptism — at least some of it! You'll notice 'testify' is used three times, indicating its importance. This part of John is in fact a series of testimonies in a daily sequence! John the Baptist testifies saying, "Here is the Lamb of God who takes away the sin of the world." Next, he says to two disciples, "behold the Lamb of God." Then Andrew to Simon: We've found the Messiah! so there is a growing realization until the final magnificent witness at the Wedding Feast of Cana.

There was this priest who loved his golf. Every chance he could get, he'd be on the golf course swinging away. It was an obsession. One Sunday was picture perfect day for golfing-the sun shining, no clouds in the sky, & temperature just right. He was in a quandary as to what to do ... play golf or say Mass. The temptation was too great, so he called a priest friend, said he was sick, & asked if he'd cover for him - which he did. He put his clubs in the car & drove three hours to a golf course where no one would recognize him. Happily, he began to play the course. An angel up above was watching him & was quite upset. He went to God and said, "Look at himself now. He should be punished for what he is doing." God nodded in agreement. The priest teed up the first hole, swung & hit the perfect drive, straight as an arrow, 235 yards right to the green, where -bingo! it gently rolled in. Every golfer's dream - A hole-in-one. He was amazed and excited. The angel was a little shocked & turned to God & said, "But, Lord, but I thought you were going to punish him. "God smiled. "I did. Think about it — now, who can he tell? "If that were me - I had no problem getting up here and saying, "Do you know what happened last Sunday?"

A man was walking by and saw a woman by her car in distress and asked if he could help. She said "Yes, my daughter's sick -I stopped to get her medication & locked my keys in my car. I must get home to her. Please, can you use this hanger to unlock it." He said, "SURE." In no time at all he opened it. She hugged him & through her tears she said, "THANK YOU SO MUCH - You're a nice man." The man replied, "Lady, I'm not a nice man. I got out of jail today where I did time for car theft. I've only been out for about an hour." The woman hugged the man again and with tears of relief cried out loud: "Thank you, Lord, for sending me a professional!"

One could talk long about the "Keys of the Kingdom", given Isaiah and the Gospel today, but I chose not -for several reasons. I prefer to talk authority in Church in the context of a scene in John's Gospel involving Peter & the Risen Lord who appeared by the lake of Galilee, where transmission of authority responsibility is clearly linked to love & humble service - Jesus saying to Peter 3 times, "Do you love me - & Peter's ardent and humble affirmation of his love - which also I'm sure it's at the heart of today's exchange!

It's not the time of year to delve into such a serious issue as we relax & cling to what's left of the holiday season. And - I'd prefer to highlight the 2nd Reading as a backdrop to Peter's profession of Faith today. We find wonderful expressions of faith & gratitude in Paul's letters - such as today's even when the topic is quite serious. We recall his dramatic- apparently instantaneous conversion -how Jesus became his Master & Lord; & while his Faith made great demands on him; yet it was no burden but an immense joy, a precious gift to share with every person.

I think this is fundamental. Scholars say Peter's confession in Matthew reflects the varying opinions about Jesus in the early Church. Paul met followers of John in Corinth, & of Silas. He was even fearful people might substitute Luke I 2.49-56. THE CHRIST-CHILD is born, says Zech, to guide us in the ways of peace (Luke 1.79). At his birth, the night sky rings with the joy of the angels, as they sing of the peace this child will bring (Luke 2. I 4). With the infant in his arms, Simeon declares that he can now "depart in peace" (Luke 2.29). The peace that the newborn Christ will impart is one of the leading themes of Luke's infancy narratives, as it is of our Christmas carols. perhaps in future this Gospel should be included in our carol services a tenth lesson tacked on to the traditional nine to remind us that the grown-up Jesus had his own ideas about what manner of peace he would bring to the earth.

"Did you think that I came to bring peace on the earth?" asks Jesus. Well, yes, Lord, we did. We believed those angels with their siren songs. We remember how you blessed people with the benediction: "Go in peace" (Luke 7-50, 8.48, 10.5—6). peace was your bequest to us at least that is what your beloved disciple said (John 14.27). We were led to expect that peace was a fruit of your kindly spirit (Galatians 5.22).

Yes, Lord, we did think that you came to give us peace. And, if you don't mind our saying so, what we are experiencing the Anglican Communion right now not to speak of Iraq is not what we thought you had in mind if this is peace, it certainly is

"the peace that passes all understanding".
The contradictions run deep, perhaps most
starkly in Jesus's apparent claim that his
purpose is to undo the work of his
predecessor John the Baptist. Gabriel had
said that it would be John's mission to heal
family divisions (Luke I . 7). Jesus' mission,
my contrast is, it seems, to foment family
division; to set close relatives against each
other. How are we to resolve these
contradictions? We harmonize the peace—
on-earth song of the Christmas angels with
the fire—on—earth warnings we shall hear
on Sunday? How do we reconcile the
scriptural promises of peace, the vision of
lions lying down with lambs, of swords
becoming ploughshares, and the rest, with
what is in fact is going on in Baghdad, in a
fissiparous Church, and for much of the

time in my own head? Bishop Edward Bickersteth in 1875 would have had us believe that "peace, perfect peace" is indeed possible '(in this dark world of sin". "The blood of Jesus", he tells us, "Whispers peace within." It is a feeble hymn, but it draws its inspiration from a great text. "Thou wilt keep him in perfect peace, whose mind is stayed on thee" (Isaiah 26.3).

There are skills by which the mind may find rest, and we have our schools of Christian prayer that teach them. There are, too, the techniques of other faith traditions, especially those of Buddhist meditation. Was Jesus a master of such methods? Did he practice "right mindfulness" He certainly slept through the storm that terrified his disciples (Mark 4. 38).Yet the evidence of Sunday's Gospel that stress I am under!") is that Jesus never achieved the unruffled serenity of the Buddha. Beneath the bodhi tree, Siddhartha Gautama found enlightenment. beneath the olive trees, Jesus embraced the cross. both paths are good, but the way of the cross is not a fast track to a quiet mind. perhaps there are things that matter more.

The good bishop Bickersteth thinks that it is both: "It is enough: earth's struggles soon shall cease, And Jesus calls us to Heaven's perfect peace." Christian spirituality has no quarrel with the quest for "peace within", nor with the hope of "peace hereafter". We are more likely to be of some use if we keep our stress levels down, and we shall be less discouraged by failure if the transient does not bound our perspective. We return this

Sunday to the great 11th chapter of Hebrews, to those whose desire for "a better country" made their engagement with the one they were in only more purposeful and effective.

What matters is that these paths — that which seeks inner peace, and that which pursues peace "beyond the river" — do not become detours to avoid the demands of the present and what is happening outside the walled garden of my own soul. The language of Sunday's Gospel is that of the prophet, the role in which Luke casts Jesus as he approaches Jerusalem. Prophets possess a still center, and they see beyond the horizon. but their focus is on the here and now. They do not agonize over the seeming contradictions between what we are promised and what we are given. There is far

too much to be done.

15

Bill, Jim, and Scott were at a Convention in Chicago where they shared a suite on the top floor of a 75-Story skyscraper. After a long day of meetings, they were shocked to learn that the hotel elevators were broken, and they'd have to climb 75 flights of stairs to get to their room. Bill said: "Let's break the monotony of this climb by focusing on something interesting. I'll tell jokes for 25 flights, Jim can sing for

A Journey Through Words

the next 25, and Scott can tell sad stories the rest of the Way." At the 26th floor, Bill stops telling jokes and Jim begins to sing. At the 51st Jim stops, Scott begins to tell sad stories. "I'll tell my saddest first," he said. "I left the room Key in the car!"

Keys are significant in The Gospel - the conferring of the power which the Keys signify the responsibility that comes with having them! Keys, especially official ones, were cumbersome then: not at all like the nifty keys to my new car!! I guess you could say Peter gets a brand-new set of keys to the Kingdom: here in the Gospel it's good to examine them! The Prophet takes the royal steward, Shebna, to task for abusing the power of the keys so it often is with leadership in the Church, which Rome seems to have ignored! (Not with Pope Francis!) Francis is the good one ! So, we wonder, how do we understand it: what impact has it on our lives in Christ? In our tradition we acknowledge that Jesus conferred a primacy on Peter that's still exercised by his Successors, the Bishops of Rome. Peter being its 1st bishop! Primacy is based on this Gospel, but not alone.

In John's Gospel there is a Resurrection story where Jesus uses deeply rooted imagery of shepherd caring for his flock to speak to Peter. As the Good Shepherd, Jesus has Peter act in His Name when he tells him to feed his lambs and the third time Jesus says feed my sheep -after Peter's third failed declaration of Love.

There's also the leading role of Peter in the New Testament in the earliest Tradition.

That we accept, day by day, where do we get our marching orders from? What influences You and I in the concrete living of our Christian faith? Many things do!

All our interactions do - if you keep in mind Jesus' words: Whatever you do to the least of my sisters and brothers, you do unto me!" And: "A cup of cold water given in my name will have its reward." This is what this scripture means to me. Our interaction with God's word present in the Eucharist- living the Eucharist 24/7.

Today: I will be mindful of my use of authority: such as it is- We all have some authority: especially in our family lives — even when we feel we have none. These parables challenge us to ask if we exercise this authority gently, lovingly, humbly with concern for the good of the other!

There are other things to reflect on when we delve into what Jesus said: though I'll not deal with them, beyond pointing out some: they'll have occurred to You, I'm sure, if you are open and attentive in your listening. Peter in reply to Jesus's pointed Question! — "Who do you say I am?" Peter, having listened to the other replies, "You're the Messiah, the Son of the Living God". This is an insight Jesus acknowledges as inspired. He then proclaims Peter blessed and confers the Keys on him: Peter has big moments, but he has his low points also. This is a comfort when we struggle to be faithful and find we slip a lot.

But Rome is far away: Pope Benedict rattling Peter's keys doesn't bother me in the morning! Though some folk outside the tradition seem to think so. Yet

it's good someone has the keys: lose our keys
or leave them behind Like the 3 guys in the
Story we'd be lost without them: in a sense,
they are even part of our identity!

So, it is! -Rome is my Family: the
main, old wise, divinely appointed! I'm glad
to belong, grateful for the shelter she affords
me: for the sense of depth and universality
she gives me: for the coherence she gives my
faith! Her severe, at times unpopular
teachings don't bother me mostly they are
needed! And infallibility means simply that
the church is a sure guide! That she
continues using those keys wisely in the
service of Christ and his people, I pray; and I
thank the Lord today for giving us that sure
guide!

16

PATRICK' S DAY 2001 AT ST. PATRICKS - WILDFIELD

I'm from County Kilkenny: the ecclesiastical division is the Diocese of Ossory. Last year, they had a Diocesan Pilgrimage to mark the Jubilee Year . Pilgrimage was very much part of the Celtic Church — we had some famous pilgrims. I think we could include Patrick himself as the first and greatest: sometimes pilgrimage is forced on us for a variety of reasons. Patrick first pilgrimage was when as a young man, he was captured by Irish raiders on the Welsh coast which was common at that time : Wales being then an outpost of the Roman Empire: it's recorded in his "Confessions" ; as is his second pilgrimage. That happened, when after he'd escaped he heard a voice of the Irish, also recorded in the "Confessions" asking him to return and bring to the Irish the Good News of Christ.

He did in the middle of the 5th century, and he was

phenomenally successful : not that anyone traveling in Ireland today might notice!

There seems to be an ebb and flow to the faith at home — and now is ebb time for a variety of reasons and we are praying for them at home. I'm praying they rediscover a servant church , because for too long the RC Church in Ireland has been too powerful, and controlled people, which isn't how Jesus operated: while he proclaimed the kingdom day in and day out, he respected peoples freedom & he became the servant of all people. There' s a famous scene at the beginning of the last Supper where he washed his apostles' feet and told them that they should live lives of simple service.

There were other great pilgrims, impelled to travel for the sake of the Good News of Jesus, Brendan, Columbkille of Iona (Columba) , Columbanus of Auxerre. The men traveled but women were prominent in the Celtic Church also: some headed great monastic communities. They say it was a wonderful period of enlightenment and it' s part of our identity, our roots.

The people who came to the Toronto Gore were pilgrims also: full of hope leaving economic misery and religious persecution for a new land; arriving here before & during the famine (as Ben Burke told us); they brought their faith with them and built their churches.(E.g. Fr. Francis McSpirritt-The miracle worker) I love this place where some of them now rest — many came from my part of Ireland; as many at St. Johns, a few miles almost due North of here, came from the North and Midlands. They speak to me of courage & great faith, and they give me hope and courage to carry on.

That's why I come here often: maybe you'll consider doing so, especially if you are young & have children. We must preserve these places as you preserved Gros Isle that Island in the St. Lawrence River where so many landed and died before coming ashore. Monday, I was on Ellis Island in New York Harbor, where 12 million people from many nations landed and were processed before entering the States: again a few million of them being our country men, in search of Freedom & Fortune.

Today is a day for us to be thankful to God for Canada and the U.S. where our ancestors found refuge and a life: where we also find refuge and a life . I sometimes hear people complain about this country: I say to them "Well then; go home". The people out there in this little graveyard didn't have that luxury! Let us be very thankful let this be our- Thanksgiving Day.

Last year's pilgrimage back in Ossory was called "Tochar Chiaran Naofa": the way of St. Kieran. Kieran is our patron saint in Ossory & they say he had an abbey at Seir Kieran, which is in Co. Leix, which is the Diocese of Kildare & Laughlin, but the parish is an island that has belonged to Ossory since ancient times.

This is the "Pilgrims Handbook" made available through all the parishes. And I'm proud to say it has a poem in it written by a sister of mine, Kitty. It' s about Pilgrimage —the pilgrimage, the journey we must make, that we' re all invited to make joyfully —the journey in time & space always mirroring the journey of the heart, where we can' t afford to clutter our lives but remain open and ready and free on the journey to God, into His

Kingdom. Kitty lives in Coventry but she' s into that kind

of thing: last year she & two other sisters, Peggie and Betty

I have 5 of them in all, still alive and going strong! They

made a pilgrimage to Iona & Lindisfarne (an outpost of

Iona connected to a great Irish saint, St.Ninian) & to

Glastonbury in Somerset where Patrick is supposed to

have stayed. I'll share her poem with you & conclude with

it & hope it speaks to you as it did to me.

May you have a wonderful St. Patrick's Day: may it lead to

a renewal of the faith that we have inherited but are called

to bring alive uniquely, each of us in our own reality in our

own time.

17

The lovely Gospel story of Mary, Martha & Jesus (Luke

10). Martha fusses & frets while Mary sits & listens

carefully; then the Lord commends Mary's attentive

listening while taking Martha to task for being too
preoccupied.

I found a like image in "Markings" a Homily Help
I've subscribed to for years. It offers a model homily for
each Sunday —often provocative. I loved this Sunday's by
Sara Miller. She opens with a similar image from the
monastery of La Grande Trappe in a remote corner of
Normandy —a Cistercian community, more human than
the Carthusian, but tough, nonetheless. Silence is big in
their spirituality —silence to listen to the still small voice
of God. They speak in Liturgy & to the animals ! She
offers this reflection that I liked.

We're often accused of being backward,
retrogressive which is way off the mark . I say —we are we
are not retro—backward but retro—cool! We' re not
circumscribed, not hemmed in by the City of Man. We
reach beyond the Wall into the City of God, in many ways.
It' s what draws us here —how we keep the batteries
charged, the oil flasks topped up! I, like many come from a
generation where we thought we had to go to mass 10

times daily & say 15 Rosaries to ensure we were in the same league as the 5 wise women. We were good but off track — for the process is more of emptying more than loading up, so we're open to mystery, to the action of God wherever it may lead —which leads me to a final sharing, a reflection I've long loved & bring out from time to time occasionally —by an anonymous person, at least now to me, but a person who surely knew wisdom, learned it the hard way, which may be the only way & who was ever—ready for the bridegroom's coming.

In imagination, we see Jesus with the Cross as his throne of Judgement, no need of words, daring us to be lovers of humanity in the raw for his sake & for his kingdom —& him gracing our efforts to be faithful. His Kingdom, he tells Pilate, the representative of Imperial Rome & all earthly powers —he makes clear it isn't of this world, and it prevails —alive & strong as is our commitment to his reign. His is a Kingdom of the Heart, Loving Service being its weapon of Choice: not, as has been said, King of Spades, shoveling dirt & abuse on people; not of King of Clubs, exerting power through the muzzle of a gun; nor king of diamonds in a realm of wealth & excess.

There have been many outstanding witnesses to Jesus's Kingdom in our time — many martyrs for Justice around the world. Oscar Romero comes to mind, & 6 Jesuits & their housekeeper, & her daughter in El Salvador, and many more. It's been said -in olden times we had martyrs who were witness to faith, today the martyrs witness justice. There's a saying of Archbishop Helder Camara, great advocate of the oppressed in his homeland, Brazil, whose compassion enveloped the world & who died not long ago: once he spoke this, "When I feed the hungry I'm called a saint: when I ask why people are hungry I'm branded a communist. "

No question - we must "give the cup of cold water in Jesus's Name." It's good to feed the poor; it's a mark of the Kingdom & it builds the kingdom across all people—made barriers of race & creed & political stripe— we'll even be praised for it by the comfortable rich whose

A Journey Through Words

consciences we soothe— but in addition —the Church's

social teaching stresses —we must be prophetic too, like

Jesus fighting the structures that perpetuate oppression.

Like Him, people are still hounded & killed— in Canada

you may be pepper sprayed! This maybe the price of

building the Kingdom. The Mystery is Jesus is still on the

Cross in a hurting child a confused adolescent, the

homeless, every victim of man's inhumanity. In our service

of them we heal Jesus's wounds, and we gain the kingdom.

It's an insight that is crucial to life, it is a gift for which we

pray. I also remember the last stanza of Gerald Manley

Hopkin's poem.

As Kingfishers Catch Fire

BY GERARD MANLEY HOPKINS

As kingfishers catch fire, dragonflies draw flame;

As tumbled over rim in roundy wells

Stones ring; like each tucked string tells, each hung bell's

Bow swung finds tongue to fling out broad its name;

Each mortal thing does one thing and the same:

Deals out that being indoors each one dwells;

Selves — goes itself; *myself* it speaks and spells,

Crying *Whát I dó is me: for that I came.*

I say móre: the just man justices;

Keeps grace: thát keeps all his goings graces;

Acts in God's eye what in God's eye he is —Chríst — for

Christ plays in ten thousand places, Lovely in limbs, and

lovely in eyes not his.

19

This tradition in Aquinas of having a Graduate

Communion Breakfast is very beautiful and meaningful, I

think. It's been there since the beginning. It was not put

there to get the Religion thing taken care of before the real

business. We are not trying to separate the secular and the

sacred; because you can't no matter how hard we try. We

are saying that one is to 'inform' or influence the other.

We want to begin the day on a proper note and let it carry

through and influence the whole day. The note is of

thanksgiving, deep gratitude to God, for all the many things we ought to be grateful for today. I am sure many speakers will touch on them before the day is over. It is a prayer also for divine guidance as we make our choices, for rich human and spiritual fulfilment.

It is a prayer for protection because it's a harsh rough world in many ways. It is, above all, an act of Worship. To be meaningful, life must be an Act of Worship and Praise. My prayer for you is that you stay in touch with your faith.

You will be very busy, your young lives going in many directions; there will be many surprises, new situations, new cities, schools, workplaces, all sorts of adjustments to make, all sorts of things to do. There will be excitement and loneliness, joy, and sadness; and there is a very real danger that the secular pursuits will take over your lives completely. I have seen it happen, often!

My prayer is that there will be a "Sabbath" a place for the Sacred, in your lives; that you will find deep meaningful quiet time for God and for things Eternal.

Carl Jung, the great German psychologist wrote the

following in "Modern Man in Search of a Soul."

"During the past 30 years, people from all the civilized countries of the earth have consulted me. I have treated many hundreds of patients, the larger number being Protestants, a smaller number Jews, and not more than five or six believing Catholics.

Among all my patients in the second half of life - that is to say, over 35 - there has not been a single one whose problem in the last resort was not that of finding a religious outlook on life. It is safe to say that every one of them feel ill because they had lost that which the living religions of every age have given to their followers, and none of them has been really healed who did not regain his religious outlook."

I think that is very significant! If I stayed with the naive faith I had when I was your age and refused to study and grow in my   beliefs, I would not be doing what I am doing now. I would be a failure, even if I did make a lot of money and was "successful" in the way Hollywood portrays success. O. J. Simpson's tragedy is precisely that:

very contemporary North American, it would appear, for all the outward achievements, he was a hollow man, poor lost soul.

Real Faith, Jesus properly understood in His Person and His Teaching, you see, doesn't take away joy. Faith in Him enriches your comings and goings; it brings fulfilment and meaning. It makes us Servants of the World and its Peoples: it opens the Mystery of the Kingdom of God. If you haven't got it, then you haven't got anything!

20

FEAST Of JESUS CHRIST, UNIVERSAL KING!

A story of a King many will recall it made a huge impression on me back then; and it still does!

School girls from the village of Beit Shemesh, near Jerusalem, were on a springtime field trip to the (so called) "Island of Peace" in the Jordan River between Israel and Jordan. Suddenly, a Jordanian soldier went berserk and started spraying the girls with automatic machine Gun fire. He chased them down a hill, killing seven and wounding many others.

CNN showed the grief in that village, bringing the images into our homes. We could not bear watching the girls being buried beneath the hard earth of their poor village: like Paris 2 weeks ago, & Beirut & a planeload of Russian tourists, from Sharm-el-Sheik to St Petersburg, falling from the skies, been blown to pieces!

In Beit Shemesh, a thing not of this world, caught everyone off guard. During grief & anguish, & anger, with no warning, the King, Hussein of Jordan, the country of the crazy gunman, left his throne, his palace, his country, & entered the homes of families of the slain girls. The King went to each of the homes & fell on his knees. He bowed down before them. In each home he looked into the eyes of the mother, the father, the sisters, the brothers, all people who were grieving the loss of their young girl & he said: "I beg you, forgive me. Your daughter is like my daughter, your loss is my loss. May God help you to bear your pain." The King, humbled before them, bowed, & walked out: back to his palace, to his country, his sovereignty! This Muslim king showed us how to live like Christ our King: it's a true story: I remember it very very well!

Today, the last Sunday of the Church Year, we Talk of Kings & Kingdoms the kingdom of God on earth and in heaven. The feast was declared by PP XI 1925. We think of tyrants Hitler & Stalin, the evil powers then: and many since! The Church would have us contrast their regimes with Christ, Prince of Peace Kings, I guess for us, are relics of the past: the word has shifted in meaning and has been devalued big time.

Now we have Burger Kings with King size burgers, the King of the Pops & the LA. kings! When the people of Israel came to Samuel asking for a King, he was against the idea. "The king will take your sons for his cavalry; He will make them plough his land and harvest his crops. He will take the best of your fields & give them to his officers. He will take the best of your cattle, and you will become his slaves." The notion of a King on his throne ruling with absolute power is one of many; Jesus stood on its head! Kings have kingdoms & palaces. Jesus left the family home in Nazareth to his mom when he became an itinerant preacher. "Foxes have holes, birds have nests, but the Son of Man has nowhere to lay his head" (Matt.8:20) Kings live in luxury. Christ had a simple lifestyle, died without a cent: even the shirt on his back was taken from him & raffled to soldiers. He died on a cross, was buried in the borrowed grave of a friend. Kings rode on horses & chariots. Christ rode a donkey Palm Sunday, the horse being an instrument of war, the Sherman Tank of its day! John quotes Zach 9:9 "Your king is coming mounted on a donkey."

Pilate asks a vital Question: "Are you the king of the Jews?" If the answer is political then Pilate & Christ are on a collision course, & the Empire has a subversive on its hands. Pilate is relieved to hear, "My kingdom is not of this world." Pilate saw through the schemes of High Priest & Pharisee, so he declared Christ innocent, washing his hands as a gesture. Then! "If you release This man, you are no friend of Caesar!" -Now Pilate himself is on trial. He declares Christ innocent, but he must watch his back. He was afraid of being reported to Rome. Christ told him to take a stand for truth; and Pilate asks: "What is truth? " (Jn. 18:38). Truth was a bridge too far for Pilate. So, he sends an innocent man to his death to save his own skin, to protect his political ambitions. "What is truth?" : it is a good Question: today the truth in TV and Newspapers is sold to vested interests, to people with agendas, to the highest bidder.

"Thy kingdom come" (Matt. 6:10) Establishing the kingdom of God on earth has been a dream of all religions. In Gaelic pre-Christian myth we spoke of the reign of the kingdom of God on earth, where "the wolf lies down with the lamb, the calf, the lion will be led by a little boy. Islam dreams of a state ruled by the Koran and Sharia law. The return to Eden on earth is a horizon never reached: the pot of gold at the end of the rainbow!

Christ won for us the kingdom: so, we wonder,

why is it not established everywhere? The answer is easy: the values of the kingdom cannot be imposed. God gave us free will. Human nature, free will, greed, and self-interest continue to thwart the kingdom of God on earth. We carry human nature around in our shoes. The weeds of sin still thrive everywhere, and we are sowing new seeds. Yet! While we may not change the world, we can change ourselves. "Thy kingdom come!" If we want to enter the heavenly kingdom, we first establish his kingdom within the bounds of our lives, our milieu. We dream of heaven: "Eye has not seen, nor ear heard what God has prepared for all who love him"!

In those ancient Gaelic manuscripts there's a story of an old man Oisin, back from Tir na Nog the land of St. Patrick, questioning St. Patrick about Christianity. Oisin wants to know if he'd hear the blackbird & thrush sing in the Christian heaven: could he hunt there as in the old days? I guess we have a different vision of heaven Oisin! Whatever it is, one thing is sure; we must establish his kingdom in our lives here first, a kingdom of love, of truth, of compassion, of justice, and forgiveness. Then one day that vision will become reality. Oisin probably discovered there's no killing in heaven -which rules out deer hunting! He may however hear the blackbird and the thrush: he'll certainly hear the birds of paradise!

Miguel Pro, Priest Martyr, was beatified by John Paul II! At 20, he entered the Society of Jesus. It was a time of political & religious persecution described by Graham Greene as the "fiercest persecution of religion anywhere since the reign of Queen Elizabeth"! His superiors ordered Miguel & the other novices to flee Mexico to California, then to Spain (1915-19). The Jesuits were banned in Spain also, so he finished in Belgium. Later he taught for a few years in Nicaragua. Ordained 1925 he returned to Mexico: where the regime Plutarco Calles restricted the Church, a fiercely anti Catholic bigot & ruthless as a cocaine cartel baron!

Miguel played cat & mouse with the police as he ministered to the people; traveling by bicycle, disguised as a mechanic, servant, a person of culture, he gave spiritual sustenance to many. He used to say, pointing to his crucifix: "Here is my weapon. With this I do not fear anyone." October 1926, a warrant for his arrest was issued. He was released next day but kept under surveillance. An attempted assassination of a former president, Alvaro Obregön, Nov 1927 was the excuse to re-arrest Miguel and his brother Roberto. A young man involved confessed his part & testified the Pro brothers weren't involved but he was ignored: though they knew the brothers were innocent, it was enough for Calles. That they were Catholic priests and so enemies of the regime. On that basis, they were condemned to die.

23 Nov 1927 - the anniversary tomorrow -Miguel Pro was executed by firing Squad. The man, responsible for his capture asked his forgiveness which was given. Before execution, Miguel asked to be allowed to pray. He knelt and prayed, then stood, stretched out his arms as if on a cross, forgave his executioners and, as they raised their guns, called in a clear voice: "Viva Cristo Rey!". When the shots failed to kill him, a soldier went up and

shot him at close range.

There's a photo record, ordered by Calles: on the front of newspapers all over Mexico - to intimidate! It misfired: it had the opposite effect - like Calvary! Now they record a martyr's death. Miguel Pro was beatified 23 Nov 1988. In many ways his story reminds me of this exchange between Jesus & Pilate, which is at the heart of the feast of Christ the King: the paradox of power, real and imaginary! Today, as we end the Church Year and begin The New, we pledge our loyalty to the source of real power: Christ!

21

Feast of the Baptism of the Lord.

To get into my Reflection on today's Scriptures and the Feast I start with the Second Reading from Acts 10; the Conversion of Cornelius and his Family, and the speech which Luke, writer of Acts, attributes to Peter. It occurs in Chap 10, exactly at the Centre of the Book, and not by co-incidence. The Acts of the Apostles hinges on this Story.

Paul has undergone conversion; he has seen the Light but was away somewhere in Asia Minor, preparing for his special work, for which this Cornelius event sets the stage.

It is transitional, with the Apostolic Church, represented by Peter, being moved by the Spirit, and responding to Cornelius earnest search. Peter's journey of Faith resembles the journey of the Magi to Bethlehem: but we are now dealing with a much more significant Epiphany, in terms of the meaning of the Christ Event for us and for all the Nations of the Earth, If you have a mind to, you might consider reading the entire chapter later today at your leisure, and chapter 11 also where Peter repeats his story for the benefit of the elders in Jerusalem; and to highlight how important it is in the larger scheme of things. Read it in the light of the significance of Baptism, the Sacrament which brings us into the sphere of Christ; sets us apart in his Service, yet makes us part of a universal religion, one writer says that Peter's vision with the resulting visit to Cornelius is essential to our theology and worship, it is a momentous occasion, this decision to baptize the Roman Centurion, Cornelius, with his household. In his speech Peter drew a direct connection between Jesus' Baptism by John and the outpouring of the Spirit on that occasion; an occasion of great significance which is mentioned by all four writers of the Gospels. Peter was a child of his Hebrew Tradition, an ancient hallowed religion, rooted in God's Revelation to Abraham, Moses, and David. Making this movement beyond Temple Worship and his narrow traditional vision was earth shattering for him. To this point he and his companions considered themselves a sect within the Hebrew religion; only at Antioch some while later is the term Christian used for the very first time (Chap. 11). It was a radically new beginning which was inescapable: there was no choice anymore because the Spirit has spoken clearly to him and to the Church. Now he, and his fellow Hebrews who were baptized, must accept the pagans and worship with them. They must even share their sacred sacrificial meal with them. I think this is very important. We all have this human tendency to put limits to the kind of people we associate with and worship with. The standards by which we judge vary. Yet we are called to a larger vision, one at once more universal and more inclusive, each time we assemble here to celebrate the great Mystery of Faith.

There is this story I read from Florida dating back about 25 years, a story of a Catholic community there, where black people could receive communion but only after the whites had been to the altar; and that Church was the liberal one! - Just about all the others were strictly segregated. The very logic of Christianity, of Baptism, is contrary to that human propensity to erect barriers of prejudice and narrowness. A few days ago I came across Nathanael Hawthorne's great old book, "The Scarlet Letter", a story of incredible bigotry and intolerance in Puritan New England. It suggests how easily religious people adopt a better-than-thou mentality, and how readily they forget the incident in Acts today, Peter's experience and the inescapable definitive conclusion: "God shows no partiality. "That's the first point I wish to make and ask that we consider. There is a second point, one I am sure has occurred to just about every one of us. It is the importance of the Moment of Baptism; and how we seem to have trivialized it and seem unable to restore its awesome significance.

You may recall the movie, "The Godfather." It's a Mafia story where, as we come to expect, the protagonists are just about all "Catholic". There's this scene, in the midst of the Murder and Mayhem, the occasion of the baptism of Michael Francis Corleone! If you've seen it and remember it, you'll probably recognize how much we sympathized with the Godfather's heroic struggle; and how, as we do with movies, we approved of his eliminating his enemies in time honoured mafia fashion; that is until the moment of the Baptism. Then the incongruity struck home, with the Godfather's affirmative "Yes, I do" to the Question, "Are you ready to help these parents in their duty as Christian Parents?"

Likewise, when called upon to renew his Baptismal Promises there is no hesitation whatever. Then he goes out, without missing a beat, to take care of some more business! It was then only that I realized he had no right being godfather to a little child who, given the circumstances, hadn't a hope of growing up to live his baptismal life as a baptized Catholic in a Christian environment. It poses a big question, I believe, for any parish. What does a Christian community do to ensure that its people, our children, will be aware of the tremendous significance of this Sacrament? It would appear that a great number want baptism merely because it gives the child an ethnic Catholic identity, or they want to ensure that the child gets into St. John Bosco school for a "Catholic Education:" meaning for many of them, in a vague sort of way, an education superior to the public system's offering. There are those too who do it to get grandmother off their case! It's a question I must ask myself because maybe I too try, like many others, not to offend people, to be the nice guy, who doesn't want to say "No", or at least "Not Yet" when I should! We baptize the babies and in a good 85% of cases, if at all, that's the last we hear of them until First Communion Preparation 5 to 6 years later: present company excluded, and I mean that! I am talking only of infant baptism; most definitely not of the RCIA program. When I was in Nigeria, we used to discuss the different approaches of bishops to the matter of Baptism. My bishop tended to be very strict and demanding; much more so, say, than the bishop of Owerri across the Niger in Iboland. Yet the Diocese of Owerri was acknowledged as the most flourishing Church in the country. Was the Bishop of Owerri wrong and the Bishop of Benin right? I don't even know if there is a question of right and wrong. All I do know is that today , you and I are invited to reflect on the scriptures, and the Feast of the Baptism of the Lord; and then, to renew our Baptismal vows with gratitude that God has favored us and made us His beloved children; then with sincere resolve we commit ourselves once more to live our Baptism within this community of the Baptized.

22

THE FEAST Of THE EPIPHANY 2016

Epiphany is a favorite festival, with the dark blue of the starry sky, the mysterious exotic Magi from the wondrous East, & the splendor of their rare and costly gifts. People's fascination down the ages has added new dimensions to the story, so that an unspecified number of wise men has become three kings, and the gifts they brought have been given defined meanings.

Artists have loved it. It's draws us deep into a sense of mystery: in the Church it leads into a season of Epiphany, of stories of Christ's revealing to the world celebrated: his baptism by John, & the miracle at Cana. The theme of the feast is revelation. All the stories are rich in symbolism: we let them play upon us; we interact with them, see what response they evoke, how they fit our life and our experience. The gifts the magi bring are symbols: we may be a bit too quick in saying what they represent. "Gold" for a king,' frankincense 'for God, "myrrh" a sign of suffering & death -these explanations that grew as time rolled on: now presented almost as a kind of fact: 'This is what it is he gets gold because he's a king, incense because

A Journey Through Words

he's God, myrrh because he's going to die.'

But scripture tells it without comment: we discover early Christians had a rich variety of ideas; it was only later it got stuck: 'We Three Kings' was ground into us as children. So today, for a few moments, we lay aside what we thought we knew. The gifts are symbols in a symbolic story, and we mustn't limit what they signify with a single 'off the peg' explanation.

Instead, we let our imagination range. Perhaps, the gifts have something to do with the Trinity. In Matthew we find this story, and he tends to repeat a word or phrase at the beginning and end of a passage to show all in between has been a unity. In the visit of the Magi we have Jesus first appearance; with people representing the wide world: how many we are not told: they have come with 3 gifts. Now look to Jesus' last words: on a Galilean Mountain, sending the disciples into the world to baptize people everywhere 'in the name of the father, the Son, and the Holy Spirit'.

If we see sold as a sign of God the father, the creator, the

137

pure source from which all things flow; the myrrh- sign of

God the Son embracing the pains and death of humanity

To heal it; and The incense -as a sign of the Spirit,

pervading all things, blowing like wind where it wills —

then we find that Jesus' first & last appearance in the

gospel speak of The Trinity, and of engagement with all

humanity, and the whole Gospel is now understood

between these identical poles.

Then we could look at it another way: the astrologers lay

down as gifts the substances they used in their divinations,

surrendering them to Christ; it isn't what they give, but

what they mean by giving that matters. They are

surrendering their life's work, their system of belief, their

sacred fools, to the Lordship of Christ. (TS Eliot's "The

Journey of the Maji" suggests this!) Their studies brought

them to him in darkness & uncertainty - but with a

glimmer towards the truth. Now they see face to face: with

no need of divination they present their tools in worship

of Christ.

St Bruno, founder of the Carthusians in the 11th

Century, saw gold, frankincense & myrrh as offering the purest of our wisdom, the discipline of our prayer, and the mortification of our lives. He said, "Thus, we offer the Lord gold when we shine in his sight with the light of heavenly wisdom. We offer him frankincense when we send up pure prayer before him, and myrrh when, mortifying our flesh with its vices and passions and by self-control, we carry the cross behind Jesus. The great Theme is revelation: revealing or manifesting Christ. What we see & find in him will be different for each of us, but if we approach with openness and humility we'll be shown what it is each one needs see. We will recognize the good we yearn for in him.

Early Christians spoke of Christ revealing afresh our true splendor, the dignity of what we are created to be. He is the perfect image made manifest: in seeing him we begin to enter upon our own healing and transformation. Some believed we must see him, however dimly, like the Magi in the story, before we can apply our wills to loving him; we must in a measure see before knowing how to love Him.

The Magi might be an image of that for us. They've sought Christ and finally found him. finding him, they have seen him; seeing him, they have loved him - and each in a different way, with a different gift to leave at his feet. We have sought him, and however imperfectly, had a sense of finding him. finding him we have, in some way, seen him. Now, seeing him, we apply our wills to loving him.

for one, perhaps, it's the gift & use of money & resources in his name; for another, a life of service to friend or stranger. One offers her mind, another his artistry or craft, another the discipline of prayer & contemplation.

Gold, frankincense and myrrh: what are they? Their meaning is as many as there are people in this world; there's no limit, no prescription. They are the frankincense gold & myrrh appropriate to the hearts of all of us who seek Christ, to all who are enlightened by his self-revelation! That we be among them, that we be wise in our time: we pray!

20

The 13ᵗʰ Sunday of Ordinary Time

Likely you haven't heard this old Gaelic rune a kind of magical poem entitled, The Rune of Hospitality.

We saw a stranger yesterday.

We put food in the eating place,

Drink in the drinking place,

Music in the listening place.

And with the sacred name of the triune God

He blessed us and our house,

Our cattle and our dear ones.

As the lark says in her song:

Often, often, often, goes the Christ

In the stranger's guise.

For me it sums up quite beautifully the message of scriptures given us, which is a call to generous hospitality: to a letting go of the self for the sake of Christ, especially

Christ as found in the needy poor. In reading one we see blessing and reward showered down on wealthy woman who took care of the Prophet Elisha; then Jesus's words "A cup of cold water given in my name will have its reward." I guess one could leave it there and say "enough" but, me being me, I won't, I want to add a little so as to stress the importance down to earth Hospitality and Generosity.

Scholars tends to restrict what Jesus says to Christians only. Those who were a poor persecuted minority in Matthew's world; this with some justification, if the Gospel stands alone! But of course, it's not alone! Consider the judgment scene in Matthew 25 and Jesus's words there- the Yardstick judgement- "I was hungry, and you gave to me to eat, thirsty and you gave me to drink, a stranger and you made me welcome... and so on" then we wonder when we did this, and we will hear. As long as you did it to the least of my sisters and brothers you did it to me.

One more story, familiar to many of you: I tell it

because Hospitality takes many forms in the mind, the heart, and the response of our entire being: A true story, told by surgeon Richard Selzer and its one that tugs the heartstrings. He tells how he had to remove a tumor from the cheek of a young woman. Post-surgery, she lies in bed, her post-operative mouth twisted in a clownish way. A tiny twig of the facial nerve had been severed, releasing a muscle that led to her mouth. Her husband is in the room along with the surgeon. The woman asks, "will my mouth always be like this?" "Yes, he tells her, "The nerve was cut." She nods and is silent, broken. But the young man, her husband smiles gently and says, "I like it, it's kind of cute." And all at once, Dr. Selzer writes, I know who this young man is. He saw Jesus in that young man Jesus in his gentleness, in his love. He says Jesus as her husband bent to kiss her crooked mouth, careful to twist his lips to fit hers, showing that their kiss still works and always will " if they receive you, they receive me." That's what the man said. The Jesus in me. The Jesus in you. The one they must see. I'd like now to repeat that Gaelic Rune; the Rune of

Hospitality; then leave it be, wishing you, and the people of this great land of ours, blessing on Canada day.

What more is there to say about Fr. Tobin?

A Journey Through Words

Ken Dobbin
The homeland awaits 👍😊 2
Like Reply 1w

Norice Millen
Such incredible memories of father Tobin! We played golf together, and i always loved going into the little Chapel, it must have been sound proofed as when you closed the door, it was whisper quiet!! Was a great place to go and decompress and recharge!! Brilliant!! 😊
Like Reply 6d   ❤ 2

> **Michelle Sullivan**
> Norice Millen Bernadette Cahill and Kathleen Hughes' fathers built it. It was very special. Don't imagine it exists anymore...
> Like Reply 5d
>
> **Norice Millen**
> Michelle Sullivan the last time I was in Toronto, I went by to see Aquinas, it was something else as they had built a new Aquinas elsewhere, i was gutted! I so wanted to walk the old halls so very much!! They would have most certainly taken the chapel away when they relocated!! That place was so special!! Life really was amazing back in those days! We just didn't know it yet! 😊
> Like Reply 5d

Caron Leid
John Wynne Thank you 😊 ❤
Like Reply 18h

Judy Brewer
I just got my copy. It's wonderful. Memories!
Like Reply 18h

Glen Speight
Wow this is super cool. How do I get one? Just go to Amazon?

Hmmm - lol - Does he tell the story about Vince Alarcon (can't recall sp)., and I, getting into a disagreement (really a fight) in the hallways at Aquinas, and how he dragged us into the chapel, lectured us (in a good way) asked us what the hell was going on, and when we weren't working with him and continued to be angry at each other, told us he was going to resolve the matter by having us formerly Box it out in a boxing ring, in the school gym in front of the entire student body? He started making calls for a boxing ring. Of course he planned to referee cause formal boxing was much more honourable than throwing punches in a "street fight" and only an Irish Priest could call a fair match. A good ole Irish Catholic way of resolving a dispute.... Honourably!

Vince A and I looked at each other after about ten mins of sitting there in disbelief, as he was planning the whole thing out, and couldn't help but break out into laughter and said no, Fr. Tobin, we're good! I mean what if one of us had lost... I'm the presence of the entire school?! Problem was solved.

Will never forget him for how genuinely engaged he was in our well being... or for him holding mass for my Moms passing in 2020, even though he had retired and I hadn't seen him in several years.

God love him for being one of the good ones in our lives.

Care Reply 17h Edited   ❤👍😊 9

Manufactured by Amazon.ca
Bolton, ON